THUNDERHEAD™

One Man's Journey
to Fulfill A Life Passion

Dr. Thunderhead

Tom Toutz

Published by Thunderhead Enterprises
tom@thunderheadonline.com

ISBN 978-0-692-32736-4

Toutz, Thomas David
Thunderhead

Printed in the United States of America

DEDICATION

My "Thunderhead" journey has been one of the most fulfilling chapters of my life. It expanded the creative side of my being. The one person that gave me undying support was my wife Linda. Her intellect, lead me on a path, that allowed me to discover my true passion for Sprint and Midget Car racing. Linda spent many years as a Marriage and Family Therapist. Along the way, she developed a theory about finding our life passion, by going back to our childhood talents and thoughts (see The Theory). She was very supportive of all of the work, travel, and energy it took to accomplish the goal. She spent many a cold evening at Ventura Raceway helping sell the Thunderhead product line to all of the fans and teams. Her charm and ability to listen, helped create more than just a vendor selling his wares. The booth became a gathering place for conversation about racing, and, most of all, about living life. She is a very powerful person. I truly love her, for all she has given me over all of these years. I dedicate this book to her.

TABLE OF CONTENTS

THE THEORY

Childhood is an experience that enlightens and prepares us for our journey forward in our lives. Beginning around the age of seven and continuing through the age of twelve is the most important stage of our young lives. My wife, Linda, spent twenty years as an MFT (Marriage, Family Therapist). Throughout her career, she counseled a vast array of clients. Most of them worked on childhood issues, that had affected their adult lives. While working with this large number of people, she began to document their lives based on the following theory: "We find our life passion between the ages of seven and twelve years of age." As a follow-up, she also researched the lives of famous people based on their obituaries featured in the newspapers. I helped with this by providing information from the pages of the *National Speed Sport News* and other racing publications. It was uncanny, as the list grew into a vast array of similar stories, all linked with the theory stated above. Famous race drivers and others associated with racing all told a similar story. At this young age, they were introduced to the sport by an important person in their lives. They were truly infatuated by the sport and all that it entailed. They were able to follow their passion, and not be detoured on life's path. In addition, she found that we are born with certain personality traits and talents. These gifts follow us throughout our lives and also influence our success or failure in what path we follow. Each of us has a talent, be it artistic talent or the ability to drive a race car. Even though we weren't born with the gene I believe it takes to be fearless on the track, we can still be part of the racing world, in one form or another, by utilizing the talent gifted us at birth.

As life proceeds, we are faced with options that steer us in one direction or another. For many reasons, which can be financial or otherwise, we don't follow that passion we had as a young child. We get caught up in making a living or raising a family. Both are noble, however, we still feel lost because our passion is not being fulfilled. Most of us continue to be a fan of racing, theater, science, art, or whatever it is that excites us. However, there is always that yearning to fulfill the passion of childhood we discovered at this early age.

MY JOURNEY

I believe life is a series of journeys that interconnect, until we leave this plane of existence. What the next plane is, I do not know, so I have tried to enjoy this trip as much as possible. My beautiful wife, who spent 20 years as a Therapist, has advanced the theory that we get our life passion at the ages of 7 through 12. She has done extensive studies of this through the years and her theory seems to hold true for almost everyone. I applied this theory to my own life and came to the following conclusion: she is correct. As a ten-year-old, I was fascinated by the Jalopy races on television. I remember watching Dick Lane call the action in Gardena, California and hounding my father to take me there in person. He did, and that was the beginning of a lifelong love affair with short track dirt car racing. I remember thinking I wanted to somehow be a part of that world. Of course, I wanted to be a race driver, until I realized later that my skill set did not qualify me as the daring type. I became a fan of the sport and have followed it ever since. Jalopies gave way to Midgets, Sprint Cars and the Silver Crown Cars, which to me were the best of the racing world. However, that passion to be part of a sport, and not just a fan, kept running through my mind as the years kept rolling by.

Being a "CAR GUY," I bought my first car when I was 15 years old. I drove it around town with no driver's license and fixed it up into a low-rider look. When I was sixteen, I got a job working thirty hours a week in a gas station at the rate of $1 per hour. Remember, this was 1958, and gas was 19 cents a gallon, and we checked your oil and tires, along with washing your windows, with a purchase of $1 worth of gas. I then asked for a raise, as I thought I was worth much more than a dollar an hour. Of course, the boss said no and I then looked for other work. This is where a life journey began, as I got a job in a men's store for $1.25

per hour when I was seventeen. I was able to buy a new car on this new high paying job and did so with the purchase of a 1960 "Bug Eye" Sprite. The job in the clothing store also exposed me to a new world of fashion and design that I never knew existed. I had been a Levi's and white t-shirt, fifties, wannabe James Dean kind of guy. Of course, at that age I was just a "Rebel without a Clue" kid, looking for a chance to do something exciting. Little did I know, that I would be in the clothing business in one form or another, for the duration of my working career. All of this, over 25 cents an hour, started a whole new journey in my life. In the clothing world, I found that I had a natural talent for all aspects of this business. It allowed the creative side of me to flourish and expand my world. The clothing and creative marketing aspects of it, have truly been a very exciting trip, that I was blessed to travel. The people I have met along the way, have enriched my life journey and blessed me with life experiences that have been priceless. If it had not been for my wife's theory, I may have missed the best journey of all. In my early fifties, we discussed the theory, and I realized that I needed to follow my true passion from childhood. Thus, the Thunderhead journey began. It flourished with a passion and love of the sport that was fulfilling beyond expectations.

The name Thunderhead was developed after watching Dave Despain on the ESPN Thunder Series on television. Each night, as he opened the show, he would say, "Welcome all of you Thunderheads out there." I realized that he was speaking to me and all of the other Thunderheads in his vast audience. Thus, I adopted the term Thunderhead and designed a logo to represent the philosophy of someone who related to our sport. My design concept was to develop a line of racing apparel that was not the typical race shirt look. I wanted something that was simplistic and more sophisticated, that, a race fan could wear out to more than just a race event.

My first event was the Chili Bowl in 1996. It was very successful, as I discovered that the design concept was enthusiastically accepted by a lot of fans out there, who were open to something new in racewear. After that, it was time to get set up with a tent and a van and hit the road to as many events as possible. My wife would tease me about the tent, because in our analysis of my childhood, another important event influenced my destiny. Around the same age of 10, the Ringling Brothers and Barnum and Bailey Circus came to Oxnard, the town in California where I grew up. I remember them unloading at the railroad station, then the Circus parade wound through town to a vacant field where the "Big Top" was erected and the show went on that night. I was fascinated with the whole operation and the performances were thrilling to watch. The next day, they packed up and hit the road to another town, where they would repeat the process. I was left wanting to be a part of something, that could be as exciting, as what I had witnessed. Now, equipped with my own Thunderhead tent, I had my own "Big Top" to set up. Wanderlust had been instilled in me at this early age.

ON THE ROAD

The sun rises as I back the van from the warehouse and hit the road for another show. Alone in my thoughts, watching the world pass by can be quite a trip unto itself. I always carried a vast array of music CDs which covered many musical genres. Music and its many forms, tell the history of our country and its people, and documents many social changes along the way. One of my favorite music styles is traditional country music that was performed in the late thirties through the fifties. These artists sang the blues and documented the trials and tribulations of everyday life experienced by everyday people. Hank Snow, Lefty Frizzell, Hank Williams, George Jones, and scores of other singers traveled the country performing for the folks. The next generation singer/song writers, like Willy Nelson and Merle Haggard, have continued this form of creative writing and singing to this day. Think back to some of the titles and singers of this era and you will find: "16 Tons and What Do You Get" by Tennessee Ernie Ford, "Jack Daniels If You Please" by David Allen Coe, and "Swinging Doors" by Merle Haggard. These songs dealt with the realities of people trying to cope with lifes anxieties. Life is not easy, so people could relate to these musical poets' work. Rockabilly entered the picture in the fifties and morphed into Rock N' Roll. Country Music today, is a combination of Rock n' Roll and Country Music. It is generally followed by the younger generations, who like their music loud, and lacking in any meaningful lyrics. Parallel to Country, we had the Black Blues, which became Rhythm and Blues and then Rock N' Roll. The next thing to hit it big was Mo Town. This unique sound gave black music the okay to play on white radio. It was a brilliant move by the record people in Detroit, but kind of a sellout to some eyes. Today, we find ourselves in the rap world of musical poetry espoused by today's youth. It is interesting to follow the career of James Brown, one of the most dynamic entertainers of the twentieth century. His style evolved from the Blues, to Rock N' Roll, to Soul Music and then Funk, which evolved into Hip Hop, and then Rap. He was instrumental in the evolution of musical taste. Imitated and beloved, by most of the performers of today's popular music, he is legendary in the music world. If you listen to today's Rap and Hip Hop, you will find anger and desperation in the writings and sounds of this generation. Sad to say, but they have every right to be disenchanted in the world that has changed so much over our lifetime. These music groups have evolved as the times changed. However, Opera is still Opera. The Big Band sound is still basically the same. Folk Music is still hanging out in a coffee house, doing similar stuff that sings of a fantasy world somewhere, that doesn't exist. Think "Puff the Magic Dragon." Jazz is still great, but not that much different than it was in the past. Yesterday's giants of Jazz, such as Charlie Parker, would fit right into today's Jazz world. As you can tell, music is very much a reflection of society and all that it entails.

Next time you travel the road, do what I do. If I am going through Bakersfield, I play Merle Haggard and Buck Owens. My thoughts can go back to their roots and migration to California of the depression/dust bowl era. As I enter Texas, it is easy. Willy Nelson, Waylon Jennings, Ernest Tubb, Kinky Friedman, Buddy Holly, Bob Wills & the Texas Playboys, Asleep at the Wheel, and numerous others fill my musical needs along that long haul across the Panhandle. After all, my father made that trip when he came out to California in the late thirties, and I would think of his journey, as I rambled down Route 40 on my way to or from the Chili Bowl. This highway replaced Route 66, an historic life changing road that was the subject of my article titled *Leaving Amarillo* which appears later in this book. Entering or leaving Oklahoma, a must stop is a visit to the Roger Miller Museum in Erick, Oklahoma. A very unique singer/songwriter, with a life story, that tells a lot about his era. Pick up a CD at the museum and then enjoy Roger and his unique style as you make your way across Oklahoma. As you can see, if you do some research, you can plan a musical road trip for each town. Not only can it be an informative journey, but, it is a lot more fun than checking your email or Facebook every 5 minutes.

Another factor in being on the road is the food issue. Unless you enjoy typical "truck stop eats," you will have to do some research. Allow a little extra time, in order to search out local eateries that do up "real home cooking." Most of these types of places are in the towns that lie just off the highway. They are worth the effort to search out, as their culinary delights can be very rewarding.

The only real exception I found to the truck stop food problem was in New Mexico, on Highway 40 at exit 208. Here stands Clines Corners, the best truck stop on the interstate. They provide excellent food, and very clean rest rooms, along with a massive gift shop, if you are into souvenirs of your travel. This place is in the absolute middle of nowhere, which makes it unique in itself. The weather in January can be quite treacherous as the elevation allows snow, sleet and ice that time of year. The first time I stopped there, I encountered a unique person on a work visa from South Africa. She was working at Clines as a waitress. She had already worked in Key West and Yosemite on her journey, and was hoping to become a citizen of the USA. We had a very interesting conversation about how life, for her, a black South African, was a great struggle. Under the apartheid system of her country, she was held back. It was fascinating to hear how she had overcome all of those obstacles and was still able to succeed on her life journey. I admired her tenacity, and willing-to-work attitude. This seems to be lacking in our country, by a lot of people who are born here. They have given up the dream and their life passion search.

Along the many miles I traveled, I found many interesting people. If you take the time to say hello, and be open to hearing about someone else, you would be amazed, at the captivating stories that are out there to be shared.

On Highway 40 is the city of Amarillo, Texas, home of the Cadillac Ranch and the "Big Texan." Both are icons of this sprawling, windblown, Texas Panhandle city. I recommend that you see them both, however, only stop at the Big Texan Steak House to look at the great interior they created. Too bad their steaks don't live up to the hype of their billboard ads that you encounter along the hundreds of miles leading into Amarillo. These offer a "free steak," if you can eat the whole thing, which consists of a giant salad, potato, bread and a giant 72 ounce steak. Only a few have conquered the task. There is, however, a great little place called the Hoffbrau Steak House. They serve up really good food that is far superior to any of the so-called steak houses that line the main highway through town. All in all, Amarillo is a real Texas town and proud of it. The journey to the Chili Bowl was always an adventure.

Heading to Knoxville on Highway 80 each August has the opposite weather of Highway 40 in January. Hot and humid, with endless miles of Highway 80 stretching out in front of you, offers little to look at when you pass through Wyoming. I did find a couple of unique places that are worth trying. In Wamsutter, Wyoming (exit 173) is the Broadway Café. It sits about a quarter mile up a dirt road next to the truck stop. This place is great, and I knew it would be when I saw the pickup trucks lined up in the parking lot. Yes, it is a dump, but the food is really good and that is what matters when you are on the road. If you go into most Wyoming towns, you will find good food located in small diners, frequented by the locals. Another great find in Wyoming is in Cheyenne. The Albany, a fixture in this old west town since 1942, serves up the best prime rib around. Everything about the place is unique and well worth stopping in for a great meal. Right next door is the Wrangler store, which is another unique operation worth spending some time viewing. This is true cowboy country.

I remember traveling with my parents on vacation in the summertime and it was always hot. Of course our car did not have air conditioning in those days, so we just had to suffer. Along the highways were always lemonade stands that offered some relief. Along with these, another form of entertainment offered weird stuff on display. "The Snake Pit," the "Giant Alligator," and others, tempted you to stop a see the weird, the bazaar sideshow type creatures of the day. One of these still remain in Arizona, on Highway 10, between Tucson and El Paso. Did I stop, you ask? Of course I did! ... Who could resist the giant billboards advertising this grotesque creature of undetermined origin? Besides, it only cost a buck and they had a Dairy Queen, so I could quench my thirst. I swore not to divulge the secret, so you will have to stop in yourself, to see this monster of the midway.

Another experience I had, occurred at 6 am at Buffalo Bills on the border of California and Nevada. I was returning from Knoxville. After 16 hours on the road, I stopped at midnight to catch some sleep. When I went to valet parking to pick up the van, the attendant took my ticket and headed off to retrieve my vehicle. As I waited and waited, I saw him slowly driving around the parking lot and I wondered what could possibly be holding up the delivery. When he finally arrived and got out, I noticed there were tears streaming down his face. I asked if he was okay. He stated that he was from Bulgaria and that I had the Ensemble of the Bulgarian Republic Choir playing on the CD. It was one track on a CD I had purchased that featured "Emmy Lou Harris' - Music that Mattered to Her," a group of songs by other artists that she really admired. By some bizarre quirk, the Bulgarian Choir song happened to play when this guy got in my van, that early morning at Stateline. He had not seen his family in five years, as he had come to America, to catch the magic of democracy, and to be able to send money home. I must say, it was quite an experience to witness. It gave me an appreciation for the blessed life that I have lived.

"On the Road Again," that famous song by Willy Nelson and Family is the first song I played when I hit the road. It describes both the excitement, and the anxiety of heading off to another big show. It did not matter where or when, as they were all great shows: The Knoxville Nationals, the Chili Bowl, Las Vegas Motor Speedway, Chico Gold Cup, the Tulare "Thunder Bowl," Skagit for the Dirt Cup and Speed Week, Manzanita Speedway, Tucson, and others. The friends made along the way were the real payoff. People, places and things all tend to fall into place, as they should, when you travel the "Thunder Road."

NATIONAL SPRINT CAR HALL OF FAME

'Promoting the Future by Preserving the Past' is the motto of the National Sprint Car Hall of Fame. Director Bob Baker and Historian Tom Schmeh head up this fine organization that is headquartered in Knoxville, Iowa. Their efforts and those of the staff are of the upmost importance in the future of Sprint Car racing as we know it today. It is imperative we all become a member of the National Sprint Car Hall of Fame. The history and future of our sport depends on all of us supporting this organization.

All of the profits from this book will be donated to the National Sprint Car Hall of Fame. I hope you enjoy the read.

Tom "Dr. Thunderhead" Toutz

VENTURA RACEWAY

VENTURA RACEWAY ARTICLES

Back in 2004, Jim Naylor, the promoter at Ventura Raceway asked me to write a weekly column for his program. As I had never really done much writing, I was, rightfully, a little nervous about accepting this challenge. However, he convinced me to give it a try and the journey began. As Jim stated, "You have a lot of opinions and stories, so just write them down," became the theme of those weekly articles. I still continue to write for his program and the challenge of meeting the weekly deadline with fresh ideas can be daunting, at times. The following pages contain some of my favorites for each of these years. Hopefully, some of the thoughts and themes will still be relevant today, as history has a way of repeating itself. It was both a challenge, and a pleasure writing them. The articles became an important part of the journey.

Ventura Raceway Articles

2004

Dr. Thunderhead

SEASON OPENER

I just can't wait, as it's been a long winter with no racing. It's finally here! The season opener at Ventura Raceway! What a season it is going to be…They say change is good and the changes this season look to be very exciting for race fans at Ventura Raceway. The VRA Sprints and Senior Sprints return along with the Dwarf Cars, Modifieds, and Stocks. Plus, the new USAC/CRA Sprint Cars, USAC Midgets and Focus Midgets will also be making special appearances.

It's a long winter, unless you are as lucky as I am to get to attend the Chili Bowl race in Tulsa, Oklahoma. This event has evolved into the premier open wheel race of the year. Drivers from across the country (210 cars this year) battle it out inside the Tulsa expo building in front of 12,000 fans. The driver list is a who's who of racing with names like Cory Kruseman, Tony Stewart, Danny Lasoski, Jason Lefler, PJ Jones, JJ Yeley, Tracy Hines, Robbie Flock, Damion Gardner, and many others, too numerous to mention. Four nights of Midget madness, culminating in a 50 lap main event on Saturday night with only 22 of the 210 cars starting. This years main was without a doubt the best ever with Ventura's Cory Kruseman taking the checkered flag for his 2nd Chili Bowl win, joining Sammy Swindell and Dan Boorse as the only two-time winners of this event.

What made it great was the battle going on behind him that brought the crowd to their feet with JJ Yeley and Tony Stewart trading slide jobs. And western states Midget shoe Danny Stratton coming from last place start to finish 7th…so much action, that it was hard to follow it all.

For a complete rundown, you can look up www.chilibowl.com where complete results and photos are available. In addition, the March issue of *Sprint Car & Midget Magazine* has an extensive article on this race. As we were leaving the Chili Bowl, the only comments I heard were, "I can't wait till next year" and "it can't get any better than this."

PASSING GEAR?

What gives with CART and this new passing gear, an electronic device used to add horsepower when needed to pass another car on the track? . . . Good grief.

The driver is allowed x number of seconds in which he can use this device during the race . . . Once the time is used up, he no longer has use of the device.

I watched the start of the Long Beach Grand Prix, in which they changed to a yellow flag lap because of a "ragged start." When the green flag flew it was "Katy bar the door" into the first corner. As always, he who leads after the first corner is the ultimate winner of the race. Passing gear, or no passing gear, it was a total sleeper from start to finish.

The IRL Race from Japan wasn't much better, a parade of cars going 200 mph around the track . . . Snore . . . Parity in Nextel Cup racing has produced the same results with most of the passing taking place in the pits. Pretty boring!

We are the lucky ones! We get to see great racing action. Side-by-side in the corners, slide jobs, amazing moves by our dirt track drivers in all divisions.

The next time you talk to a fan of these other forms of racing, invite them along to Ventura Raceway. They will truly appreciate the action on the "Best Little Dirt Track" in America...See you at the "real races."

"NICE FOLKS"

Nice Folks—You will find them sitting beside you at any Sprint Car or Midget race you might attend, be it here or anywhere across the country.

Last week, was the season opener, both here and at Hanford and Las Vegas. For me, it is reunion time, when I meet up with friends from other parts of the country.

I became friends with the people sitting around us at the Knoxville Nationals. Two are from Louisiana, and we meet in Vegas for the World of Outlaws two-night show every year. Get this: their names are BUBBA & DIXIE.

True southern folks and with true southern hospitality. We have enjoyed their friendship and look forward to seeing them each year. They are REAL SPRINT CAR NUTS.

The other group we see at Hanford are from northern California and we get together at Hanford for the opener and also the Gold Cup in September. Hanford was rained out this year, so, we will catch up with each other sometime this summer. I met them at Speed Week about nine years ago and we have been great friends ever since. We also meet up at the Oval Nationals in the fall to end the season together.

Just say "HOWDY NEIGHBOR" to the stranger sitting next to you. Great friendships await, with nice people who share a common interest with you.

THE FIRST RACE

Do you remember your first race? It was probably long ago when you were just a kid. Your parents or a relative drug you to the track and what an event it probably was . . . watching those race cars sliding through the corners, spewing fan tails of dirt into the sky, the deafening sound of open exhaust, and the smell of racing fuel filling the air. Got you hooked right off the bat and you have been coming ever since.

I remember my first race as if it was yesterday. We watched the jalopy races on live television with Dick Lane slamming his hand on car fenders during the commercials . . . We had to go see them in person. So our parents made the long trip to Gardena, with us kids in tow, to see this great event. Hooked from the get-go.

Gardena, Culver City, the Carpenteria Thunder Bowl, and Oxnard Speedway. Yes, there was a racetrack in Oxnard. It was located in the riverbed near Wagon Wheel. We saw all the great jalopy drivers including Parnelli Jones in action at these old tracks that are gone, but not forgotten. They live on in our memory of the "GOOD OLD DAYS." Well, guess what? History repeats itself and a new generation of kids we see at Ventura Raceway will someday be saying, "remember the good old days," when we are long gone.

The driver names will be different, however, the memories will be the same and the stories will carry on the tradition.

The great George Jones sang a song titled "Who's Gonna Fill Their Shoes." The lyrics asked who was going to fill the shoes of the singers of his generation when they were gone. We are faced with the same question, "Who's Gonna Fill These Stands" when we are gone?

CHEATER

Big headlines this week about Dale Jr. being fined $10,000 and losing 25 points in the Nextel Cup Series points chase for the championship. It seems that he bragged about it to his crew on the radio, which was not exactly a bright idea.

I don't think that his dad would have done this, however, the master veterans of racing probably know better…just do the deed and get on with the race.

The bigger question: Is it cheating to pull this stunt or is it just a brilliant strategic move to stay in contention in the race?

Two years ago, at the Oval Nationals, the race was for 100 laps with a break at 50 laps, splitting the race into two parts. Brent Kaeding, "The King of California" was about to be lapped as the field started lap 49… suddenly he pulled up to the top of the racetrack and slowed down. The car was jerking and seemed to have lost power. Out came the yellow flag and Brent headed to the work area where the problem was corrected in record time! The "KING" returned to the track at the back of the pack and finished the first 50 laps with a better track position. I don't remember how he finished, but it was much better than if he had been lapped. Conversation around me from fans of his that were visiting from up north contained the words—"another brilliant move by the wile old master."

So, is it cheating, or a good race move to pull off a stunt like this?

ANSWER: Beauty is in the eye of the beholder.

THE BIG SHOW

"THE MONTH OF MAY"—I remember when it was the biggest month of the year culminating in the running of the "BIG ONE" at the Indianapolis Motor Speedway on Memorial Day. I couldn't wait to hear it on the radio with Sid Collins calling all the action in such a way that one could picture in their mind the actual event as it unfolded. Then a miracle of modern science was introduced with closed circuit broadcasting of the race. My father and I went down to see the race live at the Olympic Auditorium in living black and white. There it was on a giant screen for all to see . . . what a sight!

So much has changed over the years. Now you can watch it on your own big screen TV in the comfort of your home in full color and with surround sound. Those great radio commentators with their descriptive insights are gone, replaced by the likes of Paul Page and his endless bellowing. I hate to sound like a "remember the good old days" person, however, it just doesn't seem as good as it was.

Thirty-three cars "maybe," all identical, with 33 motors, all identical, just doesn't compare with the times of the past when teams showed up with "their" concept of what would be the fastest car to last the 500 miles and win the "BIG ONE." The NOVI SPECIAL, the TURBINE, just two of the many ideas that showed up in the month of May to challenge the old school of thought. They gave the event color that is sadly lacking in today's world of rocket ship racing and nameless, faceless drivers who are all politically correct and perfect corporate front men for advertising campaigns.

So, what can a "good old days" person do? Thank goodness we still have Sprint Car and Midget racing to watch and enjoy. It is the still the best racing one can watch, so, sit back and enjoy the real "BIG SHOW."

It is still here every Saturday night at Ventura Raceway . . .

QUICK TIME

One of my favorite trips is going to Hanford to see the World of Outlaws for the season opener. I get there early in the afternoon and meet my friends at the Superior Dairy for a Hot Fudge Sunday… Superior is an old-fashioned '50s diner located in downtown Hanford, which makes the best ice cream you will ever eat. Don't miss it if you happen to be in Hanford.

It may seem strange to some, but I love to watch the whole show unfold at Hanford. Track preparation, hot laps, time trials, races. There is something about the black gumbo clay surface that makes the whole process interesting. Hot laps are done in two sessions with the second set being quite meaningful. Watching Steve Kinser and the rest of them trying different lines around the track, looking for the fastest way around is a show in itself.

A few years ago, the track was perfect and fast as lightning. Thirty cars ran the time trials and the track record was broken 11 times. Each time the track announcer would shout 'QUICK TIME' as the car passed the finish line for their qualifying run. The crowd would roar and then wait in anticipation for the next car to run. It was an exciting evening to be part of and we still talk about it today.

Qualifying runs are always a subject of controversy among race fans and drivers. Some love them and some hate them. Which is more fair, the pill draw or time trials? Tonight we will be watching the USAC/CRA Sprint Cars which include time trials to set the field. Try watching the whole show. Let the drama unfold from hot laps to the main event.

It can be quite an experience, especially if you hear "QUICK TIME."

INDY

I am sure most of you watched the INDY 500 on TV last weekend. The question is, was it out of habit, or was it because you really like INDY car racing as it is today? I remember the first live telecast in 1964, which was broadcast via closed circuit to arenas around the country. We marveled at the technology that brought this major event to us in living black and white. This years show featured camera angles from every conceivable position on the race cars and even the drivers themselves. The pre-race show was actually one of the best yet in it's coverage of in-depth information about the history and current driver/owner combinations. The only exception I would make to this was the constant picture of unshaven David Letterman chomping on his gum . . . paleeeeze . . . give us a break!!!

In spite of all this great, high tech reporting, there is something missing from the story. The human factor has been replaced by high tech machinery. Both the cars and the computers are so good that it has taken the drama away from the event. The staff of engineers can tell exactly when and where changes need to be made or fuel needs to be added. They even know when it will start raining and can plan accordingly. I miss the days when an educated guess was the norm and the human factor gave some drama that kept you wondering what would happen.

High tech drivers are another concern, as Madison Avenue has polished the current crop into corporate marching soldiers that all sound and look the same. Only A.J. Foyt remains a fading picture of the days when people said what they felt and let the chips fall where they may. He is the only "character" left to remind us of what it was like in the "GOOD OLD DAYS." . . . and good they were.

Alas, nothing lasts forever, and someday this generation will be talking about the "GOOD OLD DAYS" of 2004 because that is all they will know. So, I will tune in again next year, and so will you. Some habits die hard... INDY is one of them.

CIVIL WAR

The NORTH verses the SOUTH. In Northern California, Sprint Car racing is predominantly winged and in Southern California the traditional non-wing cars prevail. Fans are sharply divided in their loyalty to one or the other.

I, on the other hand, enjoy both forms of racing. In my travels north, I have had the pleasure of seeing some awesome shows featuring the winged sprinters at Marysville, Tulare, Chico, Petaluma, Antioch and Hanford. Winged racing is best on short bull rings like the tracks mentioned above. On the bigger tracks the racing becomes more like NASCAR with little passing or side-by-side action. I recommend you take the opportunity to see them if you are up in that part of the state.

What if we had a true CIVIL WAR showdown between Northern California and Southern California? Can you imagine the car count for an event of this type?

The South would add wings and invade Marysville for a two-night showdown with hot laps and qualifying on Friday night. Saturday night would feature heats along with C, B and A mains. The next week, the North would take off their wings and travel to Ventura for a repeat program. A true CIVIL WAR between the North and South. Points would be awarded at each event with the points added together for the two events culminating in a true "KING OF CALIFORNIA" being crowned. Throw in some major sponsorship and the purse could be big enough to make it a major event.

Some of you are probably laughing at this notion. Some of you are probably thinking I should be committed. Some of you might be right. However, dreams outside the box can be a lot of fun!

THE ROAD TO INDY

The IRL was founded and Tony George announced that open wheel American racers will now have the opportunity to advance to the "big leagues" and the INDY 500. Well, the joke is on us, as none of this has even come close to happening. He even talked USAC into calling their series "THE ROAD TO INDY." You will still see the patch being worn by their officials at USAC events!

It sounded great. We, the fans, could once again cheer on the local heroes who made it to INDY . . . just like the good old days. Alas, all that glitters is not gold, as the road took a detour to NASCAR. The "GOOD OLD BOYS" knew talent when they saw it and have rounded up the creme of the open wheel crop, leaving the IRL stuck with the elitist crowd from around the world. The only problem with this, is that other than INDY, the crowds at IRL events are nothing to write home about. Meanwhile, NASCAR continues to pack them in on a weekly basis.

Jeff Gordon, Ryan Newman, JJ Yeley, Tony Stewart, Kasey Kane, Dave Blaney, Mike Bliss and Jason Lefler have all become standout drivers in the Truck, Busch, and Cup series. Most of the above drivers appeared at Ventura Raceway over the years and Jason Lefler ran his first Midget race here. Considering the few openings available to drivers within the NASCAR circuits, this says something about the Midget and Sprint drivers ability to transfer over to other types of racing.

Each week in *National Speed Sport News*, the letters to the editor are filled with requests to have the Silver Crown Cars run at INDY in order to bring back the glory of the "GOOD OLD DAYS." I will tell you when this will happen: NEVER! The IRL, INDY, CART, are about one thing . . . big money, big egos. It has become the playground of the super rich and their toys and will remain so from now on. The "ROAD TO INDY" turned out to be a dead end.

AWESOME

AWESOME! How else could you describe the main event last week at Ventura Raceway? I have been to a lot of race tracks all over the country, but it seems to me that the racing here is the best racing you will have the good fortune to watch.

What can you say about Mike Kirby that hasn't already been said? He owns Ventura Raceway and has won more main events than any other driver in the track's history.

All of our drivers display talent and the will to win, which makes the shows very exciting to watch for the fans. However, when Kirby arrives in town, the bar is raised to a higher level that seems just out of reach for everyone else. It is similar to "Tiger Woods" on the PGA Tour. He raised the bar and it took the others five years to catch up and give him a challenge to his supremacy on the links.

Kirby will return for the "WAGS DASH" on Oct. 16 in what should make for a really great event. The "Wags" format will be different this year. Mr. Wags is planning on a couple of dash events featuring two groups of high point and low point drivers. This, along with money spread throughout the evening on other races, should make for a fun night at the races. Of course, we will all enjoy the Chili Feed and Best Looking Driver Contests, along with the silent auction and a good time will be had by all. Don't forget to mark your calendar and arrive at noon for all of the festivities. It is one event you cannot miss. Will Kirby reign supreme at the Wags Dash? . . . Be there and see for yourself.

KING OF THE HILL

The usual method for determining the starting rotation of the main events is to have a pill draw or a dash. The pill draw dictates the order for which the fastest eight cars will be inverted. This method is one of pure luck, which can result in the fastest car starting in the fourth row and if the track has slicked out, he is at a severe disadvantage for having been the fast qualifier. The dash method also favors the cars on the front row and usually is not that good of a race, as no one wants to crash out of his main event as that is where the points and cash mean the most.

At the "Front Row Challenge," in Iowa, this past August, they instituted an interesting method of determining the starting order for the eight fastest qualifiers who made it through their heat races. It was called "King of the Hill." The eight qualifiers went one-on-one in two-lap match races to determine who would get the pole. It was very exciting and the fans really got into the action on the track. Two cars, two laps, with the winner going on to meet the next winner until only one was left and he started on the pole for the main event.

This type of innovation makes for interesting situations instead of remaining with the same old methods. At one time, there was a "Helmet Dash," then the "Trophy Dash," and they evolved into the "Dash." Maybe it is time for another method such as the "King of the Hill" to replace the "Dash" in the USAC/CRA format. It would certainly be worth a try and is also very entertaining for the fans. What do you think? Let me know.

SAFETY

Last week we were treated to some great racing action, which is the norm here at Ventura Raceway. Lots of close side-by-side, wheel-to-wheel duels that make Sprint Car racing the great sport it is. Unfortunately, we also witnessed a bad accident that sent Dennis Rodriguez to the hospital. We hope he is okay and will return to the races soon.

This brings up the subject of safety, often talked about, but seldom placed at the top of a drivers list of needs. Most often, drivers are looking for a way to go faster and will spend a lot of money chasing that elusive piece of equipment that is the "ANSWER" or the "IN THING" to have on the car. In addition to parts, a bigger and fancier "HAULER" fits into this category of "MUST HAVE" items on a racers wish list. "IT WILL NEVER HAPPEN TO ME" is another excuse for not spending money on safety features that could save serious injury or worse in a racing accident.

Hello out there! . . . Time to wake up and face reality. Racing is a dangerous sport and not having the best and latest available safety equipment is just "DUMB." We, your fans, love all of you and really appreciate the show you put on for us each week. More importantly, we want to see you around for a long time to come, so give safety some thought . . . please!

I think that the most important piece of safety equipment needed in Sprint Car racing is the new seats that have been developed that are state-of-the-art in design and function. At the Chili Bowl Trade Show, Butlerbuilt featured a radical design seat, that should be a must on every drivers list of needs. The protection it offered was sensational, compared to the straight back aluminum seats, you see on most Sprint Cars. I recommend that every driver/car owner look up their website and give them a call . . . www.butlerbuilt.net. It is one call you won't regret. Think about it.

THE NATIONALS

Knoxville, Iowa, pop. 7,500. Except during Speed Week, when it swells to upwards of 35,000 Sprint Car maniacs from all over the world. Yes, Australia, New Zealand and Canada are well represented at the Knoxville Nationals, giving the event an international flavor. The big side benefit for the town is the economic impact that the crowd brings with it. Estimates are in the $10-$15 million dollar range and for a small town this is huge.

Every local group has a fundraiser going: homemade pie booths, pancake breakfast, pork and corn on the cob are sold all over town. The big hit this year was "COW PIE BINGO" where you could win up to $500 if your cow dumped on your number…only in Iowa!!

The other big one is the 50/50 drawing each night at the races. Half the money goes to local and driver charities and half goes to some lucky fan. The numbers are big, Wed. night was $5,000, Thur. night was $7,000, Fri. night was $9,800 and Sat. night was $16,000. Total Score: $37,800 each for the fans and charity.

Nine nights of racing, if you attend the whole deal split between Knoxville and Oscaloosa raceways. It is truly Sprint Car heaven as the racing is intense and car count for the Nationals was one-hundred-thirty – 410s and seventy-five – 360s plus forty-five traditional non-wing sprinters.

The event is shown live on TV for the Saturday Finals, but it is not the same as being there. You have to see this week-long event to really get the flavor of big-time Sprint Car racing. Qualifying nights on Wed. and Thur. set the tone for each driver. If you don't qualify well, you are hard pressed to make the main on Saturday. Half the cars run on Wednesday and half on Thursday, with qualifying times counting as much as the main event each night. This made for great racing as the "big dogs" Steve Kinser, Joey Saldana, and Sammy Swindell all ran the "C" main on Saturday night with Joey and Sammy missing out for the first time in years. Steve "The King" Kinser showed why they call him the "KING," with a barnstorming charge through the "B," from the back, and another charge from 24th to 7th in the main event on Saturday night. Lasoski won the event for the fourth time after dueling with Terry McCarl, a local favorite, for most of the race.

I could describe it until I am blue in the face…you just have to make the trip and experience it for yourself . . . "Just Do It." . . . You won't regret it one bit.

NICKNAMES

There is a long tradition in motor racing of giving nicknames to drivers.

These names were usually given by the announcer at a racers home track and just seem to stick with them for their whole career. I like the idea and I think it adds a little color to the whole show. Some people think it is corny, however, we must remember that racing is "entertainment" and needs the colorful addition that nicknames bring to the program.

Some nicknames from the past included: "Bullit" Joe Garson, "Wild Bill" Cherry, George "Ziggy" Snyder, Clark "Shorty" Templemen, "Fast" Eddie Sachs, Al "Mr. Clean" Miller, Richard "Red" Amick, John "Bat" Masterson, "Roll Over" Ross Olni and who could ever forget Sammy "The Flying Flea" Tanner.

Today we have a current crop of nicknamed drivers who also are very colorful characters and crowd pleasers. They include (and forgive me if I leave anyone out): Ronnie "The Rocket" Case, "Roarin'" Oren Prosser, Cory "The Cruiser" Kruseman, "Big Wave" Dave, "Gentleman" Jim Porter, and Luis "Hollywood" Espinoza. Around the country, we have Jack "The Wild Child" Haudenschild, "Slammin'" Sammy Swindell, Randy "The Hurricane" Hannigan, Danny "The Dude" Lasoski, Craig "The Crowd Pleaser" Dollansky and of course, the "KING" Steve Kinser. In addition to the drivers, we are fortunate enough to have Jim "The Mouth of the West" Naylor as our promoter/announcer.

So, should we nickname all of our drivers? . . . Let's give it a whirl. . . Email me with your suggestions and we will see what happens. This project could turn out to be a lot of fun! Along with keeping a racing tradition going for the future.

OUR NATIONAL ANTHEM

The quality of music has changed dramatically over the years, along with many other things in this country. It seems as though our standards of quality have diminished to quite a low point, especially in the field of music. Gone are days of pure voices, replaced by computerized sound systems that make a singer sound better than they really are. This is fine as long as you have the equipment at hand that can modify a voice. However, if you don't, then the audience suffers. This is especially true when it comes to our National Anthem, which is probably one of the most difficult songs to sing.

Some examples from my recent trips are as follows: An Elvis impersonator who forgot the words, a teenager, who was off key and also forgot the words. I heard a country singer who had no range and screeched the high notes. Along with these were some folks who could really sing and didn't try to overpower the song. There was a 9-year-old girl who did a very nice rendition. A woman from Knoxville who sang the Australian, New Zealand, Canadian, and American National Anthems at the Nationals with a very soft mezzo soprano voice that was just wonderful. A trumpet player at the Gold Cup, who played a flawless rendition, hitting all the high notes to perfection.

The only question I have to the management at these events is: Do you have these people audition for this gig or do you just let anyone give it a go? Please give us a break. Play a recorded version, or make sure the singer can really sing, before you book them! . . . The song deserves respect from both the singer and the audience.

FAME

Yes, fame can be fleeting, here today and gone tomorrow. In the world of entertainment, auto racing is certainly part of the entertainment world, fame becomes the by-product of success. The question: Is the pleasure worth the pain?

Let's look at some of the famous drivers of today. Steve Kinser, Sammy Swindel, Tony Stewart, and Jeff Gordon. All have reached the pinnacle of success and with it the fame and fortune that accompany it. The American public likes to build its heroes and then try and tear them down off the pedestal they put them on. Just attend a WOO race and you will hear 2/3 of the fans cheer for Kinser and 1/3 boo him. The split for Sammy is more 50/50 and also more vocal. At the front row challenge in Iowa this year, Tony Stewart was in attendance and appeared after the main event along with Danny Lasoski, his WOO Sprint Car driver. A portion of the crowd became boo-birds and for the life of me I just don't get it. Here is a guy who grabbed the gold ring of success but has not forgotten the world from which he came. He remains a very important part of the Sprint Car world. His active role in sponsoring several drivers in cars he owns has provided them with career opportunities they may not have found elsewhere. Compare this to Jeff Gordon, who also caught the brass ring, but never looked back once he reached the top. Jeff "Long Gone" Gordon would be a good nickname for him.

Fame is fleeting and also brings with it the hardship of living up to everything the public expects from its heroes. Fame comes with a price tag that not all can deal with once they achieve it. The following statement is by my favorite author/songwriter, Kinky Friedman. I think it tells it like it is, for those who reach the so-called brass ring.

"For those few who find lasting fame within their lifetime,
Things can be sometimes even more frustating. If you think
It's hard living with who you are, try living with who you've
Become."

Ventura Raceway Articles

2005

Dr. Thunderhead

FAMILY TRADITION

An often asked question is "how do these drivers get involved in racing?" For many, it is from being around the sport from birth. One such family is our own Clark Templeman III.

His family history goes way back to the very beginnings of USAC in the early fifties.

Clark's grandpa, Clark Thomas Templeman, also, known as "Shorty," was a very famous USAC Midget racer, and, in fact, won the first outdoor race at Bonelli Stadium (later known as Saugus Speedway). His career included three USAC National Midget Championships in 1956, 1957 & 1958. He won five Washington Racing Association Championships from 1949 through 1953, the USAC Midwest Championships in 1956 & 1957, three Oregon State Championships, and, in 1956 won three event features in one night at the "Night Before the Indy 500." In addition, he raced five times in the Indy 500 between 1955 and 1962 with a 4th place being his best finish in 1961. Sadly, he was killed in a Midget crash at Marion Speedway in Ohio in 1962, leaving behind a wife and four children.

One of his children, Clark Thomas Templeman Jr., continued the tradition and took up Sprint Car racing on the west coast. He was the CRA Rookie of the Year in 1970, finished 2nd in points to Jimmy Oskie in 1974, won the Pacific Coast Nationals and the Salute to Indy Races in 1974. He won a total of 15 CRA main events, two USAC National Sprint main events, one being at El Dora which he won from the back row, and he represented Team USA in South Africa in 1974. Clark Jr. perished in a fatal Sprint Car crash at Ascot, in June of 1982, leaving behind two children and a close friend who happened to be his ex-wife.

Our Clark Thomas Templeman III, began his race career as a Go-Kart racer, winning three Championships along with 30 main events.

He was ranked 9th in the nation and then took on the Sprint Cars in 1997. He has won several main events and, along with his wife Tammi and son Mason, runs his own team in the VRA series, whenever finances permit.

With the cost of racing today being so high, it is not easy to run as much as they would like, but they are having fun with racing being a hobby and not a total way of life.

Family tradition, yes, for the Templemans and several other family groups we see at the races. Is it "in the blood"? . . . I say absolutely . . . In spite of experiencing tragedy and hardship, the tradition rolls on from generation to generation. I wish them all the best in their pursuit of the "thrill of victory." It must be an awesome feeling, that satisfies some inner desire, that only a few get to experience.

READ ALL ABOUT IT

I was asked recently about where one can find news about Sprint Car and Midget Car racing. Good question, as most sports pages cover the stick and ball sports as if they were the only sporting events happening.

The major southern California papers, the *L.A. Times* and the *Daily News* both have writers covering motor racing. However, I guess they never leave the office, as both papers only write about major racing leagues such as NASCAR, IRL, Cart, Formula One, etc. An occasional paragraph at the end of their columns might mention Ventura, Perris or Irwindale when they need to fill space on a page. What part of "reporting" do these "award winning" reporters not understand? It would be nice to see them covering the local racing scene where the stars of tomorrow get their start.

Our local paper, the *Ventura County Star*, has the results of each Saturday nights events on Sunday morning in the sports page. This is fine, however, it would seem that racing in Ventura, being a major part of the local sports scene, would have some in-depth coverage on a weekly basis. Papers in northern California give their local tracks, much more coverage, including front page space for the bigger events.

There are three excellent options for getting the news on our sport, they are as follows:

NATIONAL SPEED SPORT NEWS: Weekly newspaper covering all forms of racing. Bi-monthly supplement titled "*Elbows Up*" covering Sprint and Midget Car racing. Subscribe at www.nationalspeedsportnews.com.

SPRINT CAR & MIDGET MAGAZINE: The premier publication of our sport. A monthly magazine devoted to Sprint Car and Midget racing with articles for both the fan and racer. Of special interest are the articles on the history of our sport. This is a must-read for anyone interested in Sprint Car and Midget racing. Subscribe at: www.sprintcarandMidget.com.

FLAT OUT MAGAZINE: An excellent publication which features several of the top writers covering the sport of Sprint Car and Midget racing.

These columns feature a wide variety of the history and current events of our sport. They also publish two other magazines titled *Dirt Modified* and *Dirt Late Model*. All three versions are published quarterly and do an excellent job of covering the sport. Subscribe online at: www.threewidemedia.com

HALF FULL OR HALF EMPTY

WOW! Can you believe it, the season is half over, and it seems as though it just started.

I always look at things as though they were half full. A half empty attitude only brings about negative thoughts. This leads to an unhappy lifestyle. So, with the season half full, let's recap what makes it half full, and not half empty.

CAR COUNT: We have enjoyed big car counts which make for great racing. Last week there were over seventy cars in the pits divided between three classes. Where can you see this action? No where, but here. With the exception of major events, most tracks are lucky to have half the cars that ran here last week.

RACING: What can you say, the racing has been fantastic, with great competition each week. It seems the program gets better each week. Our main events have been literal slugfests with a different winner taking home the glory each week. Last week was a great example. Ronnie "The Rocket" Case literally bulled his way through the final laps to take the win.

What will the second half bring? I am sure that after the FAIR break, we will continue to have great action. September 2/3 brings the finals of the Grand Slam series. This will be a two-night show featuring drivers from the north coming down to battle our local guys. A real North/South "CIVIL WAR." USAC Sprints and the Wags Dash are also on the calendar later on. Sounds good to me! I can't wait for those great shows, as they always provide terrific racing.

I am taking off for the Knoxville Nationals in August. This is always a great trip, nine nights of Sprint Car action at the big half-mile in Knoxville, Iowa. On the Road Again, keeping that glass half full ... See You in September...also, two of my favorite songs.

STARTERS

The World of Outlaws announced that starters will be required for the 2006 racing season.

You could hear the roar of outrage across the country from sea to shining sea! How can this be, they ask…the cost will be outrageous… car counts will dwindle … only the rich will be left … and on, and on, and on.

Truth is, starters would probably be a godsend to Sprint Car racing as it is currently run. Red flag time would be minimal, cars could start and continue without drawing a yellow flag, and cars could get on the track in much less time to start the race. This would speed up the program, which is always a good thing.

However, tradition plays a big part in Sprint Car racing. We are throwbacks to the good old days, and we like to keep it that way. God forbid we should have some changes that might make for a better program. I guess I am one of those who like it the way it is. I watched a George Strait concert that was filmed two years ago. During the concert he sang a song titled, "Murder in Music City." The song told of present day management killing off the fiddles and steel guitars, from the current crop of country singers, and turning country music into a rock n' roll format. It was done in order to expand the market, and capture a larger share of the consumers dollars. I guess it must have worked, as most of the big groups today, in country music, do not have these two vital instruments in their bands. That is why I only listen to the old stuff, as it is more real, and more interesting, than the current crop of young guns in the music world.

There are three things that can speed up a program without adding starters. First, no open red flags. Open red flags, are nothing but time killers, and, penalize the racer who set it up right from the beginning. Second, one-way radios from the control tower to each driver. This would allow the lineup to get ready much faster than the current use of a hand written sign. Third, tracks need to adopt the Chili Bowl method of lining up cars for each race. The cars are pushed out onto the track, by the crews, and the push trucks get them started in no time...you have to see it to appreciate its expediency. It really works, and it gives the announcer time to introduce each driver before the noise level is too high to hear him. Call me old fashioned, or a traditionalist, but, these three improvements would make for a better program than starters.

JUST IN THE NICK OF TIME

Wow, Tony George must be doing handstands after his big event on Memorial Day.

Danica Patrick rode in on a white horse and rescued the INDY 500 with a 40% increase in viewers over last years dismal showing. She was the most exciting thing to happen at this event in years. She has it all: talent, looks, personality and charm. Just what the doctor ordered, to bring some life into the ailing patient, known as the IRL. It will be interesting to see if this new interest will carry over to increased viewers in future IRL events.

The telecast, this year, was a good one in most areas. The absence of Paul Page was a plus, even though he was replaced with Brent Musberger. Brent must have a lifetime contract with ABC and knows little, if anything, about racing, so go figure. The absence of Bob Jenkins, a true expert on racing, was a big mistake in my view.

One could detect a changing of the guard, based on interviews held by the pit reporters.

Not one interview with A.J. Foyt. In years past, his opinion was held in high regard and this year, he was not to be found. He has been replaced with super teams consisting of big buck operations and unlimited funds. This has left Foyt and the rest of the field in the position of field fillers. NASCAR suffers from the same problem. Both leagues are compiled of 'the haves' and 'the have nots.' This is not going to bode well for the long term health of racing as we know it.

So, was it worth watching? Absolutely, it was a great show!
TRIVIA QUESTION: WHO WON THE 2005 INDY 500?
ANSWER: WHO CARES.

LEGENDS

Muhammad Ali in boxing, Michael Jordan in basketball, Elroy "Crazy Legs" Hirsch in football, Pele in soccer, Babe Ruth in baseball. The list goes on and on, featuring the greatest of all time, in every major sporting field. One wonders what makes a legend stand out in their respective field. In my mind, it is when they cross a line that sets them apart from others in their field, setting standards that most cannot achieve.

Parnelli Jones is a true legend in auto racing, and, we have the pleasure of honoring him today at our annual Wag's Dash. I am one of the fortunate ones to have watched him run in many forms of racing. Beginning with the Jalopy races, on good old black and white TV, and onward, through Midget, Sprint Car, Indy Car and Stock Car competition. A race with Parnelli was always thrilling to watch and he was always the "one to beat" in any form of racing.

In addition, his two sons, P.J. and Page were part of legendary Midget racing during the ESPN series at Ventura Raceway. No one can forget the epic battles they staged during that great period of Midget racing history, right here at our track. In addition, the "Jones Boys" battle at the Chili Bowl is still talked about today, and will be for many years to come.

So, who will be the legends of the future? . . . Sit back and watch tonight's program. You might just catch one in the making.

THE BIG LEAGUES

"What went wrong?" you ask. Why hasn't Sprint Car/Midget racing become the premier type of racing events in the country. They are, without a doubt, the most exciting form of racing today, and have been, since they began many years ago. It is mind-boggling to see, what other forms of racing have risen to, in terms of dollars and prestige.

In 1953, the Hoosier Hundred, was run at the Indiana State Fairgrounds. Imagine this, the purse was $22,240, with an additional $3,010 in lap prize money. This amounted to being the second biggest purse next to the INDY 500. If you factor in inflation, the purse would probably be around $1,000,000, in today's dollars, maybe even more. Over eighteen-thousand fans crowded in to watch the event.

USAC ruled the racing world in those days. The INDY 500, Champ Cars, Sprint Cars, Midgets, and Stock Cars. But, their luster has gone by the wayside. No longer the sanctioning body for the 500, or the Stock Car game. NASCAR took over the Stock Car racing world and drove it into one of the top sporting events in the country. Try as they might, it never clicked for USAC. They remain a grass-roots organization, with many various regional series splintered around the country. Even their national series is mainly in the midwest, centered around Indiana and Ohio. Just imagine what a dynamic marketing program might have brought to this great sport.

The World of Outlaws, whether you love them, or hate them, is the only true national Sprint Car series alive today. They travel the entire country and race before packed grandstands at every stop. From January to October, over 50,000 miles, with a true national champion crowned at the end of each season. They are the closest thing we have in Sprint Car racing to being "big league."

So, is it really that bad, not being one of the big league sports? Not really! We get to watch great racing, without having to put up with all of the TV requirements and inflated ticket prices, etc., that go along with it. Maybe Sprint Car and Midget racing is better off as a grass-roots thing. Yeah, but what if?

GREEN-WHITE-CHECKER

Two weeks ago we were treated to one of the best senior main events ever.

The cause of this exciting race was a green-white-checker race that evolved into a battle in lapped traffic. Ron Porter, the "senior statesman" of Sprint Car racing put on a show to behold for the fans in the stands.

Ron is one of the most exciting drivers to watch in any division. His rim-riding style is a sight to behold. Fearless, in his execution of a three car pass to take the lead through turns three and four, he brought the fans to their feet. The crowd roared their approval as he held on to finish his first main event victory. Congratulations to Ron, and thanks for a great show.

Ron drove his first race, a Midget event, in his native New Zealand in 1949. In those days, there were no roll bars or seat belts, so, you know he is one brave guy. He continued with a career in auto racing highlighted by working with Carol Shelby. He was crew chief for the Cobra GT40 and was with the Shelby team five times at Le Mans during the 1960s.

For the last 10 years, he has driven the "Flying Shingle," in antique car races at places like Laguna Seca. This car was developed by the late Ken Miles and I was fortunate enough to watch Ken race it at Santa Barbara, Pomona, and other southern California sports car venues during the late '50s and early '60s. It was based on a MG-TD chassis with a very modern body style. It was truly a joy to watch.

Ron is an outstanding competitor, and, a pleasure to talk to. At age 71, he has a real zest for life and a great attitude. We are looking forward to more main event wins from this hard charger.

CHANGING TIMES

Yes, times, they are a changing! Each year goes by, and things are not what they were the year before. Sometimes we get stuck talking about the good old days and how great it was back when! Maybe it was better, and, then again, maybe it was just different. Who knows? But, things still change.

Look at the national standings for Midgets, Sprint Cars and Silver Crown Cars. Jay Drake, Josh Wise, Bud Kaeding are all battling for supremacy in these divisions. Not long ago, we were watching these California guys do battle at Ventura, and other speedways in California. The racing was great and all of them put on terrific shows for us on the west coast. However, times change, and they all moved on to further their respective racing careers in the USAC national rankings. The racing we are watching today is just as good, and maybe even better, than it was back then. The events we've had this year will go down as the "good old days" in a few years. One just has to realize that times change and go with the flow.

Tonight, we will bid a fond farewell to one of the "good old boys." Wally Pankratz, part of the "good old days" and also part of the present, will say farewell to Ventura Raceway.

Yes, he will be missed! He is, in my opinion, one of the all-time best racers I have had the pleasure of watching over these many years. Wally has always been a "gentleman racer" and a most gracious individual in both victory and defeat. Thank you, Wally, you will be missed by me and all of your many fans throughout the country. Best wishes to you in all of your future endeavors.

THE THRILL IS GONE

Yes, BB King, the great blues artist moaned out the blues with his great hit, "The Thrill is Gone." You can just feel the pain in his voice as he sings this great classic like no one else can.

This Memorial Day, the INDY 500 will be run again, but, is the "THRILL" gone? I would say that for the most part it is. If you watched the time trials last weekend, it was quite evident that the thrill is gone for the spectators as the crowd has dwindled for "Bump Day" to just a smattering of folks scattered along the front stretch. I think we will probably have more fans in the stands here tonight than they did for their traditional day of qualifications. Several years ago, the place would have been packed for this important day.

The announcers were trying their best to make us believe that "drama" was building. It seemed that every five minutes they would go down to the pits and use the word drama in trying to add some excitement to the telecast. Well, it wasn't to be found except in their imagination. Try though they might, it just wasn't there.

I am sure the event will have a huge crowd on Memorial Day, and yes, I will watch it as I do every year. Some habits are hard to break, especially one I have spent a lifetime doing.

Tony George and his merry band of IRL owners have lost touch with reality and the tradition that made this such a great event. It is sad to watch this happen. Little do they realize that the result of their decisions has resulted in removing the "thrill" from the month of May. Yes, 'THE THRILL IS GONE" should replace "BACK HOME AGAIN IN INDIANA" with BB King singing it during the opening ceremonies.

WINNING

If you go back in time, racing was held up to seven nights a week. Drivers could actually make a living being Midget and Sprint Car pilots at the multitude of racing facilities that existed in every town up and down the state. This condition also led to the top drivers accumulating a large number of main event wins. Drivers like Johnny Boyd lost track of the number of features he had won. Being interviewed by *Sprint Car & Midget Magazine*, however, he did recall one stretch at San Jose when he won 12 of 15 features. He went on to race at INDY from 1955 to 1966 and his Midget/Sprint Car career spanned from 1945 to 1966 when he retired after the INDY race in May of that year.

In today's world, a driver might be able to race 25 times in a year. This pales in comparison to racing five to seven nights a week, so winning a large number of main events is not an easy task. Our program tonight features the USAC/CRA Sprint Cars and the field contains quite a few multiple main event winners. Rip Williams, always a fan favorite, recently won his 100th main event in a career going back 25+ years. He is close on the heels of breaking Dean Thompson's record of 103 career wins and should be able to accomplish this goal by the end of this season.

Winning this amount of main events is something most drivers can only dream about. It takes exceptional skill, great equipment and of course racing luck, to rack up this many wins. Of course, it is said, you make your own luck and I think this is true to a large extent..

The Ripper's elbows-up driving style has thrilled fans for many years. So, sit back and enjoy watching his quest to pass the 103 wins that the great Dean Thompson posted. It should make for a great show.

INITIALS

NFL, MLS, NBA, MLB, NASCAR, IRL, NHRA, PGA, LPGA, ETC., ETC., ETC. Today, these stand for most of the major league sports in this country. Big bucks and TV rule the roost in all of these sports. Each of these have evolved into giant marketing machines. Their initial purpose is now overshadowed by the advertising of major companies, looking for market share, in their respective fields.

Guess what? We now have the NSL—"NATIONAL SPRINT CAR LEAGUE." The latest attempt to take Sprint Car racing into the big leagues along with the above mentioned groups. Another split, with the Pettys, dividing the World of Outlaws by forming a new league. Remember CART vs. IRL? . . . Does no one learn from past mistakes? . . . Are the massive egos in today's sporting world so large that they think it will work. Time will tell, I guess. Let's hope it works for the best.

Sprint Car racing, even the big leagues of Sprint Car racing, has always been a grass-roots sport. If you mention Sprint Car racing to the average person, you normally get a puzzled look on their face, along with a statement such as, "I've never heard of it." Or, they say, "You mean NASCAR!" You then have to try and explain our sport, which is not an easy task. Sprint Car racing is a sport you have to see to believe. No amount of explanation, or TV, can truly explain it. One must attend a Sprint Car event to get the real exposure needed to understand it. So, the next time you are asked, "what is Sprint Car racing?" . . . Bring them along with you, to a race, and let it explain itself.

DIVORCE

According to Webster's Dictionary: The legal termination of a marriage. The complete separation of things. Divorce is an ugly thing to go through. Sometimes it starts out in an amicable way and then turns into a war zone. We see this in many celebrity marriages and they even made a movie about the subject. Lots of press about the battle over assets and of course, the kids.

The divorce between the SCRA and the tracks they appeared at, was no different than that of many marriages. A lot of hurt feelings, angry words, and the complete separation of the parties involved.

Of course, the ones left with the most pain were the children. The children, in this case, were the many fans of Sprint Car racing. Forced to choose between which parent they would stay with, the SCRA or the new USAC/CRA division. It was a tough choice for many, and the split is still evident, based on the fan count following the split. A lot of familiar faces no longer appear at both the front and back gates. I miss them, as they were a good bunch of folks, always here for the big 410 shows, packing the grandstands with enthusiasm. Maybe someday they will return, maybe not, but we all lost something with that turn of events.

The USAC/CRA show has gone on to become the dominant series in 410 racing on the west coast. The last I read about the SCRA was an eight car main event at Chowchilla in their 360 division, which doesn't look good for their future. Time marches on, and lives are changed forever, when divorce enters the picture. Let's hope that some form of reconciliation brings the lost children back into the fold. I miss them, and I bet you do too.

BEST SEAT IN THE HOUSE

Many years ago, I was with a company that produced Hang Ten imprinted t-shirts and socks. One of our advertising campaigns was a sponsorship of World Team Tennis, which at the time, was riding the crest of a tennis boom across the country. One of the perks of sponsorship were seats at the Forum for all of the World Team Tennis events.

Our seats were in the corner of the court, not on the center line. At first, I thought that we were being slighted in seat selection. However, I soon realized that they were the best seats in the house. We could watch the match without turning our heads constantly to follow the ball.

At Perris, I sit in turn four for the same reason. I can see the whole track in one viewpoint, without turning my head constantly, and missing part of the action. Last Saturday, I gave turn one a try, for the main event, with the USAC/VRA Sprint Cars. What a view! ... I could watch the whole field at once! It was quite interesting, as I could see the various lines the drivers were taking, and the various strategies being used to make passes. Racing consists of offense and defense, and I could really see it take place from this vantage point.

Most of us sit in the same seats week after week. Sort of a habit, that is hard to break, because it is comfortable, and comfort feels good. Well, I recommend that you break the habit, and give turn one a try ... It is "THE BEST SEAT IN THE HOUSE."

GRAND SLAM

Wow, the "Grand Slam" is here at last! No, not the Denny's version, but our own big event. The culmination of racing at four different tracks ending in a two-night show at Ventura Raceway.

An event of this stature has been long in coming, and it fills a real need. Sprint Car racing is a patchwork quilt at best. Race tracks are spread out over a large geographical area and are run by very independent promoters. These promoters are interested in attracting, both paying fans and large car counts. Both increments are necessary in order to keep the gates open, and, to hopefully show a profit. It took a Herculean effort on the part of Cliff Morgan to put together this series. Balancing the wants of four different tracks and two different associations required great political maneuvering on his part. In spite of all the problems, Cliff managed to pull it off, so sit back and enjoy two nights of great racing.

Most everyone saw the film, "Field of Dreams," and the message "build it and they will come," that the film portrayed. It is true, and, it happens more often than not. Some examples in our sport are: The Chili Bowl. Emmett Hahn, in 1986, started what is now the biggest open wheel race in the country. People told him he was crazy and that it would never fly. After losing money for five years, it took off and will celebrate its 20th running next January. The National Sprint Car Hall of Fame is another example, along with the Knoxville Nationals. Both being in a very small town in the middle of nowhere, yet the people came.

Having a vision, and the perseverance to see it through, can bring great rewards. Let's hope that the Grand Slam becomes another Chili Bowl in the years to come. Our sport, and our region, need an event series of this stature.

THE NATIONALS

Twenty-four Sprint Cars, Four Abreast, Twenty-four Push Trucks, Three Abreast. Here they come in the Salute Formation down the front stretch at the Knoxville Nationals. The culmination of three nights of furious competition, between 120 Sprint Car teams, from all over the U.S., Canada, Australia and New Zealand. Standing among the crowd of 30,000 fans, anticipating the start, is one great place to be.

Twenty-thousand horse power is unleashed at the start as they scream into turn one. This event is the one race that every Sprint Car fan should attend at least once. Whether you care for winged racing or not, the Nationals should be on your "A" list of things to do. It is not just the racing. It is the whole week of events surrounding the Nationals that make it special.

The town of Knoxville is mobbed with race fans, vendors and race teams. It is really a circus atmosphere and everyone has a great time. A visit to the Hall of Fame is worth the trip itself. Here you can delve into the history of this great sport. Tom Schmeh and staff have done a superb job of preserving the past for all fans to enjoy. Craig Agan, of the Hall of Fame, is trying to include Ventura Raceway on his next west coast trip. Hopefully, he will be here in early September. We look forward to his visit.

As the main event ends, it is goodbye to all of the friends I have made, until next year, when we will meet again. The Nationals—You Gotta Love it.

Ventura Raceway Articles

2006

Dr. Thunderhead

TRAGIC LOSS

The Sprint Car world has lost one of its most important figures with the tragic accident that took the life of Fred Brownsfield. The veteran race promoter was killed by a race car at his Grays Harbor Raceway in Elma Washington, June 16th, while lining up the start of the D feature, for the Northwest Modified Nationals. His passing, has set the Sprint Car world, in a very precarious position. He was the head of the new National Sprint Car Tour that resulted from the split with the World of Outlaws.

A very successful driver in his early years, Fred went on to become one of the sports top promoters, and a highly respected person in the racing world. When the NST was formed and quickly folded, as the Pettys pulled out, it was Fred that took charge and rescued the fledging league from certain failure. Through his leadership, and business acumen, he was able to establish the new tour in a very short period of time. The NST was well on it's way to becoming a viable entity in the racing world. The future of this tour is now in great jeopardy, as it will be a struggle to keep it going. The most likely scenario will be a reconciliation with the World of Outlaws.

Whatever the outcome, it is a great loss both to his family and the sport. This is just another reminder of the dangers involved in the racing world. Anything can happen, at any time, as time and again, these freak accidents occur. It is imperative that all of us, yes, even fans, be constantly aware of what is going on around us, as accidents do happen.

Safety has to be the number one priority for everyone involved. Be SAFE.

STATE OF THE UNION

I made my annual trip to the Oval Nationals at Perris Auto Speedway last weekend. It is always a lot of fun, as I mix it with golf for three days, and renew old friendships, with many of my fellow Sprint Car fans. The event has grown to be one of the top traditional Sprint Car events in the nation, pitting the best-of-the-best, from the east and west. A true national meeting of top teams from across the nation, doing battle for the $30,000 top prize.

All things considered, Sprint Car racing seems to be having a great year. Car counts are up, with 75 cars checking in for the Oval Nationals. Fan attendance was good, with a sell-out on Saturday night along with decent crowds on Thursday and Friday. The racing on the preliminary nights was as good as it gets, with great action both nights leading up to the showdown on Saturday. A dry, slick track Saturday night played into the hands of Dave Darland, who put on quite a show battling Tony Jones for the victory.

One thing stands out in my mind concerning the future of Sprint Car racing. The average age of most of the fans attending appears to be over 50 years of age. This is not a good state of the union for Sprint Car racing. USAC and all other racing associations need to be promoting the sport to a younger crowd if they expect it to grow, or even maintain its audience base. This problem will reach a crisis stage if something is not done, and done soon. The future of the sport is on the line!

THE END IS NEAR

Yes, the season is winding down, and will soon end for another year. It seems to go by faster every season. The opening night seems to have been run a few weeks ago. Maybe I am just getting old, but time is flying faster and faster each year.

The points chase is very interesting this year for the VRA series, with several drivers still in contention, and only three events left on the schedule.

This brings up the question of having a NASCAR-style chase for the last ten races of the season. I, for one, would be against it. I think that it does not reward consistency throughout the season. The championship should go to the driver who is able to put together a total season of strong performances.

The chase erases all of the efforts that a driver and his team put together, and the season basically starts all over again. NASCAR is using it as a sales tool, to compete against football and baseball, which compete heavily with their TV ratings in the fall of the year. The PGA has the same problem and will probably adapt a chase-type finish in the years to come. Local racing is better off without a chase system.

RUMORS

I love the rumor mill! Countless articles appear in both the regular press, and the newspapers and magazines that are devoted to the racing world, concerning the merger between the IRL, and Champ Car. If you believe the press clippings of the last year, then it would seem that the merger is right around the corner.

Nothing could be further from the truth. You will never see a merger between these two groups, because this is a divorce that cannot be reconciled. Just today, the *L.A. Times*, ran another article with pictures of both Tony George, and Kevin Kalkhoven discussing the dim hopes of the two leagues getting together. At the end of the article they left open the slight chance that something may happen in the future. They forgot the most important fact that rules the situation. EGO—yes, if you look at the pictures of these two giants of the racing world, you will see massive ego written all over their faces. Neither one of them will be willing to give up their throne for the good of open wheel racing. Not now, and most certainly not in the future.

Where does that leave us, the fans, in the equation? Right where we need to be, watching Sprint Cars at Ventura and other tracks we might attend. We know that our drivers will never be seen in either of the "big leagues" of open wheel racing. Maybe that is good! After all, we get to see the better racing than the IRL or Champ Car can offer, even on their best day.

VINTAGE CLASSICS

I had the pleasure of touring the Otis Chandler Museum of Transportation this week. The museum is closing. All of the cars and motorcycles will be auctioned off on October 21st. Otis was quite a collector of extremely rare items, gathering only the best of breed. Of course, it helped, that he was born into the *Los Angeles Times* family, and the untold fortune that came with it. Regardless, he still managed to put together quite an array of classic stuff that was a pleasure to view. One wonders if he truly wanted it to be sold off at auction, or would he have preferred to have it live on as his legacy.

In today's automotive world, almost every car has a similar look. They are designed in wind tunnels to achieve maximum gas mileage, ending up with the same look. Chrysler has taken a bolder route, with their blunt nosed styling and retro look, that at least gives the consumer something different from which to choose. In the era of classic cars shown at the museum, each designer had their own idea of how a car should look. They were each an artistic masterpiece of hand-tooled beauty.

Race cars of today also have a similar look, with off-the-shelf designs that must meet certain specs. Gone are the days, when a Watson Roadster stood out in a crowded Pit area, along with many other designs, that were unique unto themselves. Yes, those days are gone, but not forgotten, by a rapidly diminishing group of oldsters. It is just evolution, working its way through time, leaving us all behind, with the relentless ticking of the clock.

WINGS VERSES TRADITIONAL

I just returned from my annual pilgrimage to the Knoxville Nationals and the Sprint Car Hall of Fame. As usual it was a grand affair with lots of ceremony and big money on the line to the winner. First place pays $140,000 and starting the main event on Saturday night pays a minimum of $7,000. One-hundred-thirty cars were entered and after three nights it boiled down to the top 24 vying for the most prestigious trophy in all of Sprint Car racing. Donny Schatz, after many 2nd place finishes, finally put it all together and won the "big one." The event was shown on live TV, so I hope most of you caught it, as it was a really good show.

Sprint Car racing has, for years, been split between the traditional (non-wing) Sprint Cars, and the winged versions. The World of Outlaws rule (for the most part) the winged cars, and USAC is the major domo of the traditional or non-winged cars. Fans of each type swear that their type of racing is the best. Winged fans don't go see the non-wingers and the non-wing fans could care less about the winged versions. I like them both for their unique styles of racing, and can argue for both sides.

The big difference I see is in the marketing of each group. The winged drivers, on the major circuit, are racing for much larger purses, than the USAC drivers. Most World of Outlaw events pay $10,000 to the main event winner. In addition, there are several shows that also pay bigger purses in the $40-$50,000 range. Meanwhile, the USAC traditional Sprint Cars are still running for traditional purses that have not increased much over the last twenty years or so. Ted Johnson, the founder of the World of Outlaws, really put Sprint Car racing on the map. In spite of his many problems along the way, he made it possible for a driver to be a true pro and earn a handsome living. He did this all by himself, while the entire USAC organization stood by and did nothing to further the image of Sprint Car racing. Marketing, you see, is the key. He raised the bar, and made the public willing to pay more, for his high perceived value show. Maybe USAC will someday wake up and join the parade.

HALL OF FAME

I have written before, about my favorite Sprint Car trip, which is to the Knoxville Nationals. The thing that makes the trip so great, is my visit to the National Sprint Car Hall of Fame. Inside this building, is the complete history of all the greatest drivers, cars, and racetracks, that have comprised the history of this great sport.

The work that the staff has done is just incredible, and each year there is something new to take in. This year it was the installation of the old ASCOT steel display of the 19-18-17- second club. They have it up on the wall and it is quite a sight to see. Thinking back to all of the drivers we saw at ASCOT brought back great memories. This is what the Hall of Fame is all about, preserving the past glories of the sport, and promoting the future.

Last week, Craig Agan, representing the Sprint Car Hall of Fame, paid us a visit. It was his first time attending the races here, and he was very impressed with the racing, and the fans in attendance. You, the Ventura fans, donated a record amount for any track he has visited, without actually having the Sprint Car being raffled, on display. Craig called to say thank you for your support, as it is truly appreciated.

We will not be in attendance this week. We are taking a little vacation to Chico for the Gold Cup. We will also be participating in the annual Gold Cup Golf Tournament which raises money for the National Sprint Car Hall of Fame. See you back here, September 16, for more VRA Sprint Car action.

THE MISSING LINK

Last week we ventured up to Chico for the annual Gold Cup Race of Champions. As usual, it was four nights of great racing, with warm weather, and good friends around us.

The annual Hall of Fame Golf Tournament was also a lot of fun. Unfortunately, our team missed the set up on the golf cart, and the cart paths were dry-slick . . . oh well, we had fun, and we helped raise $300 with our sponsorship of a par three closest-to-the-pin deal.

The Gold Cup seems to bring out the best in competition, and this years field of 115 Sprint Cars was no exception. Each night provided spectacular racing with hard fought battles to see who would make the main on Saturday night. The main event this year paid $50,000 to win, and along with the prestige of being one of the top five races in the country, it was quite a show. Daryn Pittman pulled off an upset over the rest of the WOO travelers and locals who made the show.

Only one thing was missing! The green car of Steve Kinser! Due to the split of the winged Sprint Car group, he and his protégé, Tim Keading, were not in attendance. Last year, they put on a real dog fight, and the fans went wild over the show. This is the price you pay when egos get in the way, and you end up with two racing sanctions. Until he retires, Kinser, will always make a show something out of the ordinary. When he hits the track, all heads turn in his direction. There is something magical about him, and the aura, that he brings to the track. Long live the King, but it would be better, if he were back with the World of Outlaws. Not just for him, and the rest of the NST, but for the good of Sprint Car racing.

OLD TIMER

I stopped by Jack Walkers shop the other day to take a look at his restoration of a 1947 Kurtis Midget. Jack is 78-years-young and a former Midget driver from the 1950s. He is in the process of restoring a 1947 Kurtis Midget, which, in the 1940s and 1950s, was the dominating Midget car. He is also a member of the WRA (Western Racing Association), and participates in their travels to various tracks to show off the cars of yesteryear. This Kurtis is powered by a V-8 60 Flathead. He hopes to have it finished in time for the Turkey Night Grand Prix. It should be a beauty to behold when he debuts it in November.

Jack drove in an era when Midget racing was the king of sports. They raced five nights a week at Gilmore, Balboa Park, San Bernardino, South Mountain (Phoenix), Tucson, Oildale, and various other tracks in southern California. This, while also holding down a regular job, must have been a grueling schedule.

This era was also full of danger, as the cars had no roll bars, or seat restraints. Many drivers were killed or seriously injured while participating during this era. In Jack's office, is a photo of him, going over the wall, at San Bernardino. Jack flew out in one direction, and the car sailed off into the parking lot. This resulted in a year of rehab before he could again race the Mighty Midgets. Fortunately, he survived this era in one piece, and is still with us as a living piece of racing history. In my travels, I have found that the racing world is full of nice people. Having the chance to talk "racing" with Jack Walker, was one of those special moments.

THE CIRCUS

I just love the circus. I have loved it since I was a little kid, when Ringling Brothers, Barnum & Bailey came to Oxnard. They unloaded at the train depot and the elephants towed everything out to a big vacant field near the airport. We watched in awe as the Big Top was set up and everything was being prepared for the big show that night. And what a show it was! Lions, tigers, the flying trapeze, clowns, and all the daring acts that made up the show. Some things just stick with you forever, and the circus is one of them for me.

I took my grandson, who is 7-years-old, to Circus Vargas, which was at the fairgrounds a week ago. It was great! Watching him look in amazement, at the various acts that made up the show, was worth the trip. Especially, the daring people who fly on the trapeze, with no fear, as they execute their intricate maneuvers. He was just awestruck with this portion of the show. It is the main event at the circus and they are the stars of the show. Even though the circus is not as big or extravagant as it once was, it is still great fun to be there.

Gone is the sideshow and all the ferocious animals that once made up the event. Some say it is for the best, however, I wonder if that is true.

Car races used to have a sideshow for big events. Joey Chitwood and his daring stunt drivers would thrill audiences with their stunts. Motorcycle riders would crash through a burning wall of flame. Motorcycle jumpers and other daring acts of bravery were part of the draw that brought fans out to see the races. Just like the circus, the sideshow is no longer a part of the show . . . some say it is for the best, I wonder if that is true.

MADE IN THE USA

A long, long time ago, the cars on the NASCAR circuit were actually the cars you drove on the street. Ford, Chevrolet, Oldsmobile, Buick, Chrysler, Hudson, and others, all used the theme of "Race on Sunday, Sell on Monday." Winning meant a lot to the different brands involved. Fans rooted for the brand of car they drove and customer loyalty was really something. My dad only drove Fords, while Linda's dad only drove Buicks. This was common in those days.

Those days have changed! The Big Three let it all go south by not bothering to stay up-to-date with "features and benefits" to owning one of their brands. In crept the Japanese and German car manufacturers, with better quality and styling. Today, you find the Big Three, scrambling to catch up. The problem they face, is, that it is easier to get a new customer, than get back one you lost. Anyone in business will agree with that statement.

Now, Toyota has entered NASCAR and the uproar among the fans is almost comical. The letters to the editor in *National Speed Sport News* decry the entry of cars from foreign companies. The Toyota trucks are leading the truck standings and the next step will be the Cup races. I guess these fans don't realize that we are now part of a global business community, and it will never be like it was. These same fans, that write in wanting only American cars in NASCAR, are probably the same ones shopping at Walmart. At Walmart, they are buying goods and services that mostly come from China and other Far East countries. What happened to their "buy American" philosophy? . . . I guess when it affects their wallet, exceptions are okay.

BOXING

Back in the '60s and '70s, boxing was a big deal in Los Angeles. The Olympic Auditorium was a hotbed of boxing activity with fights televised live every Thursday night on local TV. The fights consisted of mostly local fighters with some coming out of Mexico. They were, however, some of the greatest fight nights in the history of boxing.

Ray "Windmill" White, the fighting carpenter from Ventura, "Indian Red" Lopez and his brother Danny "Little Red," Frankie "Too Sweet" Jennings, Raul Rojas, Jerry and Mike Quarry. These and other colorful fighters packed the local arena every week, putting on great shows for the locals.

All of them dreamed of making it to the big leagues of boxing, Madison Square Garden or Las Vegas. Jerry and Mike Quarry both made it, on live title fights from Las Vegas against Muhammad Ali and Bob Foster. Both Jerry and Mike were knocked out by their opponents in devastating defeats on national TV. Sad to say both brothers suffered from pugilistic dementia with Jerry passing on seven years ago and Mike passing on this week, both at an early age. Boxing sometimes has a stiff price to pay for the fame involved.

What does this have to do with racing, you ask? The fights at the local arena were better than the big deals at the Garden or Vegas. Just as today's local racing is a lot better than the big leagues of NASCAR, IRL, CHAMP CAR, or FORMULA ONE. Just attend a race at Ventura, Perris, Chico, Santa Maria or Tulare, and you will see some of the best action anywhere. Better than any of the big deals on TV, which have become mostly boring round-de-rounds. Fame in racing also has a price to pay, the loss of fun. Just ask Tony Stewart why he always returns to run the Chili Bowl. He does so because it is still pure fun to be there. No obligations, just great racing.

SPRINT CAR & MIDGET MAGAZINE

I just can't wait for each issue of *Sprint Car and Midget Magazine*. Without a doubt, Doug Auld has put together a terrific publication, focusing on our sport of Sprint Car and Midget racing. This months issue is probably one of the best ever with the usual columns and latest racing updates.

One article that is a must-read details the life of "Iron Mike" Nazaruk. A child of the Great Depression and a true World War II hero, he went on to be one of the great drivers of the '40s and '50s, until his untimely death at Langhorne in 1955. He raced everything from Midgets, Sprint Cars to Indy Cars. The photo of him in 1954 in one of the great roadsters reminds us of this great era of Indy Car racing. There was something special about the design of this era of Indy Car. There was also something special about the men who raced them. Fearless, death defying, or as Mike was tagged "invincible."

However, no one is invincible, not even the great Mike Nazaruk. We must remember racing is a dangerous sport. It was even more so back in "the day" when men like Mike ventured out in machines that were primitive at best. His quote in April of 1955:

"Nobody's invincible. Way I see it, I've been on borrowed time since about the second day at Saipan," certainly rang true for him.

This article, along with others, is what makes *Sprint Car and Midget Magazine* a must for every fan of the sport.

THE MONTH OF GRAY

Gray clouds have been covering Indianapolis for the month of May. Rain has plagued both practice and qualifying sessions. Just what Indy needed to go along with the lack of entrants and interest in what once was the "Greatest Spectacle in Racing." It seems a shame that such a great event has dwindled down to just another race because of the massive egos involved. It is probably too late to salvage, even if they merge back with CART.

Without the entries of a few old timers, Andretti, Unser and Cheever, they would not have filled the field. The race is now dominated by a few multi-car teams that dominate the rest of the also-rans. I think that the cost of racing at this level has contributed in a large way to the demise of the series. A steering wheel on one of these rockets costs $25,000. Without major corporate sponsorship, it is impossible to field a car with any chance of being competitive with the top teams.

ABC Sports had their hands full trying to make the Qualifying and Bump Day dramatic.

It is not an easy task to build drama when no drama exists. The absence of Bob Jenkins in the announcer booth also left a lot to be desired, as he is without a doubt the best there is in analyzing open wheel racing. He is currently heading up the new Silver Crown series that I wrote about in a previous article. Let's hope he returns some day in the future as his commentary is always a pleasure to hear.

"The King is Dead, Long Live the King," certainly fits the current state of Indy Car racing.

SNOWPLOW

Big Cars, Champ Cars, Silver Crown Cars. The names have changed over the years, but, until this year, the cars were always built on the same basic concept. This made for a good opportunity for a low budget race team to participate, and not go bankrupt. Winning wasn't the most important goal for this group. The racing was fun and filled the need for speed. I have spoken with several teams over the years and that was their philosophy. The division gave them a chance to be part of the game. I have watched this series at the Indiana State Fair Grounds, Irwindale, Cal Expo, and Del Mar. The old design was fun to watch . . . like being in a time warp.

All that has changed with the introduction of the "new" design. Intended to bring USAC drivers to bigger tracks, and more exposure to NASCAR. The goal of USAC is to have the Silver Crown division be a feeder series. Of course, only the well-heeled need apply.

This, of course, has resulted in another split, with a new association being developed to run on all of the tracks USAC dumped for this new endeavor. Will it ever end? Splitting an already small pie serves no real purpose except the self-serving egos at USAC.

Last, but not least, the new design looks like a high tech snow plow. I guess USAC, being from the Midwest, figures the drivers can pick up a few bucks in the winter, pushing snow around.

HORSEPOWER

A unit of power is equal to 745.7 w or 33,000 ft.-lb per minute. That is the description in the dictionary. Our Sprint Cars put out around 650 horsepower depending on who is doing the talking. The 410s put out around 850-900 horses, also depending on who is doing the talking, or should I say bragging.

The obvious question: How much power does a horse have?...We will find out this weekend at the Kentucky Derby. Twenty-two horses will square off in the Derby which will be shown via satellite at the Derby Club right next door. Like Formula One, the Indy 500, Daytona, or other major sporting events, the Derby is a major event attended by more than 150,000 crazed and drunken fans. A ticket to the Derby is one of the top 10 tickets in the world of sports. Seventy-five thousand of these people will be in the infield, where they will not even be able to see the race. It is like most things in life, those that have the scratch, get it, and those that don't, don't. The Derby is a great American tradition!

One of the traditions at the Derby is the wearing of creative hats, some of which go back 100 years. Hats have been passed down from generation to generation and are one of the key elements that make the Derby unique.

This sparks a great idea: I now proclaim Saturday, July 1st as "HAT DAY AT VENTURA RACEWAY." Get your creative juices flowing and create your own unique hat . . . we will have PRIZES and a HAT PARADE . . . this should be a blast and may even start a great tradition . . . I CAN'T WAIT . . . GO FOR IT!

FORMULA $$$$$$$$$

$350,000,000—YES, that is the budget for Ferrari Formula One racing in the year 2006.

It is mind boggling, to say the least! Just think, it is more money than the total gross national product of many countries and a lot of major corporations around the world.

I watched the Italian Grand Prix last weekend, if for no other reason than to see what all the fuss was about. Considering the amount of money spent, I was rather shocked at the lack of real racing that took place. The first part of the race was based on the amount of fuel in each race car. The announcers made a big deal about how the pit stop timing would affect the outcome of the finish. No passing, just follow Michael Shumacher around to the finish. The most drama occurs on pit stops, where 18-man crews change tires and fuel the car in under eight seconds.

Michael is the second highest paid athlete in the world and will earn approximately one billion dollars over his career. Only Tiger Woods is paid more to perform in the sporting world. Big money, along with all of the banners and national pride of the countries involved give Formula One major event status. Like most major events, they don't hold a candle to the real racing we get to see here at Ventura Raceway. So, sit back and enjoy the best racing action you will see anywhere . . . right here . . . Sprint Cars on the dirt . . . it doesn't get any better than this!

HALL OF FAMER

Louise Smith, a pioneer of stock-car racing and the first woman inducted into the International Motorsports Hall of Fame, has died. She was 89. Known as a fearless, hard charging driver, Smith competed in the 1940s and 1950s alongside the men who were the early stars of NASCAR. She won 38 races in various classes over an 11-year stretch while barnstorming tracks from Florida to Canada.

Smith grew up in a family of mechanics and was drawn to cars before she was a teenager. She was known as one of the fastest drivers in the area, one who enjoyed outrunning the police. Of course, if it were today, those chases would be on TV with the whole world looking on. Times have certainly changed, although not for the better.

In 1946, Bill France Sr. came to Greenville and was looking for a female competitor to attract fans to the track. Someone mentioned Smith, and that was the start of her racing career. She finished third in a modified 1939 Ford coupe in that first race. Smith raced for another decade with drivers such as Lee Petty, Buck Baker and others. "I was born to be wild," she was quoted in 1997 by the *Baltimore Sun*. She had tried to be a nurse, a pilot and a beautician and couldn't make it as any of them. "But from the moment I hit the racetrack, it was exactly what I wanted."

What a great story! In an era when women were not allowed in the pits or a race car. Relegated to roles as trophy queens, she managed to achieve stardom in what was then strictly a man's world.

THE OFF SEASON

Every sport has a season. Football starts with spring training and ends with the Super Bowl. The same thing with baseball: spring training, the regular season, and then the World Series. Hockey runs through the winter and ends with the Stanley Cup playoffs.

Basketball has a longer run, leading to the playoffs. This leaves my three favorite sports, auto racing, golf and horse racing.

Somehow, the participants and fans of these three sporting events can't get enough of a good thing. Of course, I think this is great. Being able to follow one's passions on a year-round cycle of good times is tough to beat. The horses run at Santa Anita, Hollywood Park, and Del Mar on a continuous cycle. Golf can be played or watched on a year-round basis. A never-ending circle of great sporting fun. Auto racing has now moved to an eleven-month cycle, with only December being out of the loop. Oh well, 11 out of 12 isn't so bad.

Sprint Car and Midget Car race fans get a bountiful array of special events throughout the fall/winter months. The Oval Nationals at Perris, followed by Manzanita's two-day show, and the Turkey Night Grand Prix fill up November. Following these events, we get the Chili Bowl in early January. The Midgets run at Phoenix in the Copper Classic, followed by the winged Sprinters at Tulare and Las Vegas. Without skipping a beat, the Ventura Raceway season is now upon us. Welcome to the best racing action anywhere, right here at the "Best Little Dirt Track" in America.

READ ALL ABOUT IT!

Last Saturday, I had the pleasure of selling the programs for the night. The program has an all new format and is quite an improvement over previous years. I suggest you read it and enjoy all of the information it provides.

Being the "hawker" for the evening was a blast...It reminded me of my paper route that I had when I was eleven years old. I grew up in Oxnard, and at that time, newspapers were the main source of news for one and all. Oxnard had the *Press Courier* and Ventura had the *Star Free Press*. Of course, the jobs at the *Courier* were all taken and I could only get the Ventura paper route. Talk about a tough sell, an out-of-town paper was it. However, I persevered and learned a lot about sales. I sold the "features and benefits" of the more diverse news that *The Star* offered at the time.

Needless to say, I was a car nut at that young age, and needed the money to buy a car...Which I did at age 15, even though I did not have a driver's license. You could get away with a lot more in those days, which brings up another thought. My dad said I could buy any car I wanted, as long as I paid for it myself. Today, it seems every kid has a new car, paid for by their parents. What kind of life lesson is that? "Ask and you shall receive" seems to be the order of the day. Parents, today, need to take a close look at this current practice. Try giving your child a life lesson, instead of a free ride.

Ventura Raceway Articles

2007

Dr. Thunderhead

SEASON OPENER

Welcome back! . . . It is race time again at Ventura Raceway. This will be the 30th year that Jim Naylor has promoted racing at Ventura Raceway.

Congratulations to Jim on this achievement. It is rare that any business stays around for 30 years, especially one in an industry that is fraught with failures all across the country. Promoting racing is a very difficult task at best, so, we are fortunate to have this venue and all that it represents.

It seems that the racing season is almost year-round. Our last race was in November of 2006 and it was followed by the Turkey Night Grand Prix and then the Chili Bowl in early January, along with racing in Arizona, in February. In reality, if you are willing to travel, the off season is about one month. I caught the Turkey Night Grand Prix, the Chili Bowl, and the big USAC show at Manzi. Attending these other venues was a lot of fun and the racing was great.

If you missed the banquet, we awarded the Thunderhead Rising Star Award to Brandon Thomson. As usual, the voting was very close. We will be looking forward to running this program again this year. Look for our list of drivers to be announced in June.

I will have more comments and views on racing as the season progresses.

Meanwhile, sit back, relax, and let's GO RACING!!

NEWS FLASH

Eight-year-old Joey Earnest, Jr. Dwarf Car driver at Ventura Raceway, has been signed to a Driver Development Program for Chip Ganassi Racing. Lorin Ranier, who heads the program says, "We feel like we can pick the guys and then we just need to put them in our system and provide them a quality place to showcase their talent." That's our philosophy. Driver development projects can provide tremendous advantages for the racers selected as well as the teams employing them. Joey will be the youngest among 50 young men and women currently involved in development programs run by more than 20 NASCAR teams. Gibbs Racing stated that they did not want to be too late in signing Joey, and he will raise the bar for other racers.

JUST KIDDING! However, the rush to develop younger and younger talent seems to have gotten out of hand. Kids leaving high school to play in the NBA and young drivers signing contracts at age 16 robs them of the pure pleasure of just having fun in life. Why must everything be about becoming the next Super Star?

Let's hope the parents of our Junior Racing program don't get caught up in this syndrome like Little League did several years ago. So far, it looks as though the Jr. program is all about fun for the kids, the fans, and their families. Keep it that way and everyone will benefit.

LAS VEGAS

We just returned from a visit to "Sin City." Yes, it is back to it's original theme. "What Happens in Vegas, Stays in Vegas," has replaced the failed "Family Friendly," atmosphere they tried a couple of years back. I, for one, knew it would never work. Baby strollers and casinos just don't mix. However, you have to give them credit for coloring outside the lines in trying to get people to visit.

Downtown has a massive four block light show with a sound system that literally blows you away. They are featuring a ten minute ad/show that features the upcoming Las Vegas Grand Prix. I must say that it was spectacular, to say the least. Cars, drivers, and logos all streaming above us, with a sound-track that was very impressive. Once again, thinking outside the box, tempting you to come back for an exciting event of speed, danger, and colorful people.

Only true race fans, of the Sprint Car culture, will know that the Champ Car World Series is not that exciting. Colorful? Yes. Exciting? Not a chance.

However, Vegas, knows how to sell the "SIZZLE," even if the steak is a little on the tough side.

NIGHT AND DAY

I realize that NASCAR is the major domo of auto racing. They own the audience on television and the marketing machine that drives it is immense.

However, when compared to the IRL telecast this past weekend, the difference was night and day.

Let's start with the NASCAR telecast. The opening segment, with Waltrip playing the plaid-coated car salesman, was pathetic at best. This was followed by their usual interviews, which are as boring as watching wallpaper dry. Then comes the Boogity, Boogity, Boogity race call and constant dribble trying to make it look exciting. Sorry, but I just don't get it! Who is it that they are catering to? The lowest common denominator seems to be their guideline.

Jump to the IRL telecast. What a contrast in style and substance. The opening graphics and introduction of the drivers and teams were stunning.

Both announcers did an incredible job of both interviewing and commenting on the race at hand. It was a sophisticated operation from start to finish. Especially, since they had a rain delay, which really put the pressure on the announcing crew. My hat's off to the IRL. Let's hope they can maintain and possibly build the league back up to the level it once held.

USAC & THE MIGHTY MIDGETS

Yes, the USAC Midget Cars are featured tonight! They have been my favorite form of open wheel racing on Bull Ring tracks. In my opinion, they are a perfect match and create some of the best racing one can observe. One feature is the diverse assortment of motors that run the series. No other series has this diversity, and that gives the Midget Cars a leg up when it comes to competition between the teams competing in this series. With the addition of Toyota motors this year, it only expands the competition further.

USAC, itself, is also very diversified. From Midgets, Focus Midgets, Sprint Cars, Dirt Silver Crown to Pavement Silver Crown, they offer a wide variety of car types across the country. Along with this diversity comes a lot controversy.

The new pavement series, featuring the ugliest race car ever designed, seems to be USAC's latest fiasco. Racing at NASCAR events on Friday afternoon, before a vast expanse of empty seats, is a sad sight to behold. The big dog's at NASCAR convinced them that the series would be a winner, but, a loser it is.

We all make decisions in our business life that we come to regret. I have found, cutting your losses early in the game, is the best decision. Chasing your losses in this new creation, is no different, than chasing your losses at the craps table . . . you end up losing it all. USAC should give it up, and return to what they do best.

SUPPORT

As we sit in the grandstand and read our program, a lot of visual advertising is at our disposal. Take a look around the track and you will see billboards.

These, along with our program advertisers, are an important part of keeping this raceway in business. Our advertisers are one of the key elements that allow us to enjoy this great sport. Without them, our racing program would suffer.

I have stated in the past, that Ventura Raceway, in some ways, is like a Country Club of Motor Sports. We pay our dues each week, and the club provides great events for us to enjoy. Compared to a Country Club, our dues are quite low. This brings up the point, of our supporting the various businesses, that support our racing. When you need a product or service, and it can be provided by one of our advertisers, give them the business.

Don't run off to a Costco and try to save a dime or two! It could cost you in the long run with a higher dues at your Country Club. When you do visit one of our sponsors, it is important that you mention their support of the racetrack. This brings the relationship full circle, and with your support, the circle will be unbroken. Enjoy your club, it is a rare entity.

RETRO

We often hear fans say they want it like the "Good Old Days." Well, we do have one race driver, who still lets it all out! Tony Stewart is the "Poster Boy" for all those fans, wanting more honest comments, about the state of racing in today's world. Tony has become a "Retro" version of A. J. Foyt. He says what is on his mind, with no regards to the consequences. It is refreshing to hear the truth, instead of the bland rhetoric, we have to endure from the rest of the bunch.

His latest "trashing" of NASCAR's debris on the track brought a $10,000 fine and a staged apology from Stewart. No doubt, it will not be the last honest comment we hear from Tony. He is always there to state his "truth" to the fans.

Tony Stewart and A. J. Foyt have a lot in common. Both are brash and bold in their statements, and usually follow it up, with great performances on the track.

A. J. has had a storied career and Stewart seems to be following in his foot steps. They even look alike, and if Stewart keeps eating at the fast food joints, he will no longer fit in a Midget. Just like his hero, A.J.

50 YEARS

I will never forget the first Sprint Car race I attended. A.J. Foyt, Parnelli Jones and Mario Andretti fighting it out on the dirt. No mufflers, no power steering, no roll cages! What a sight to behold, it was. Just sheer courage, by all three men, as they battled for victory. Those days are gone forever, but one of them, A. J. Foyt is still at it. He will celebrate his 50th year at Indy with this years' running of the 500.

Both as a driver, and car owner, he has proven to be the toughest, and most outspoken of them all. There is A. J.'s way, or the highway, when dealing with this icon of motor sports. In today's world of political correctness, only Tony Stewart even comes close. Most will agree that he is a clone of A. J. Foyt, and the rest of the bunch all bow down to their corporate masters.

A. J. Foyt was the King of Bricks, having won four times, competing in 35 consecutive starts, led the most races with 13, and finished nine times in the top three, with top 10 finishes totaling 17. What a record! And, he did it in an era without the luxury of today's life style in racing.

Tough as nails, you bet! However, you got to love him, for who he is, and what he stands for . . . There will never be another!

"BIG DEAL"

Memorial Day is here, and where did the time go. It seems as though the season just started, and now it is almost half over. I don't know about you, but this rapid rate of passing time, is getting to be a bit much. The month of May disappeared like a tornado.

So, here we are, and the Indy 500 is on for another year. Unfortunately, we are faced with the same old story. What happened to the "Greatest Spectacle in Racing?" It is now a shadow of its former greatness, lacking the "Star Power" that it once held. The "Fans" have spoken! The management of the Indy Racing League have not listened, and so, they are left with an elitist event. This, is far from what once was an event, that everybody looked forward to with anticipation.

Will it ever return to being the premier racing event of the world? I don't see it happening in the near future, if ever. In any business, you have to give your customers what they want, not some ego driven fantasy of your own.

That said, will I watch? Yes, of course. Old habits are hard to break. Maybe it will be a great race, in spite of all the damage inflicted by Tony George, and his merry band of elitist ego maniacs.

RAIN

The Indy 500, or in this year's case, the rain-shortened version, is over for another year. What was developing into another great finish, was tarnished by a long rain delay, and then a deluge, that ended the show early.

Winning a rain-shortened Indy 500 is somewhat of a hollow victory. It is the case of being in the right place at the right time. There will always be an asterisk next to the winners name that takes away some of the glory that accompanies being on the Borg Warner Trophy. Missing, is the finish line, being crossed at over 200 mph, with the crowd of 300,000 people on their feet.

No driver really wants to win the Indy 445, or the Indy 462. It is the Indy 500, that sets it apart, from any other race in the world.

As we have seen many times this season, at Ventura Raceway, a lot can happen in those closing laps. That is what brings us back each week, hoping for another finish of the complete race, not a shortened version. The thrill of victory at the finish line is what it is all about.

LEGENDARY

Every time race fans gather, the subject of legendary tracks seem to arise.

It seems that every region has one, "the track to end all tracks." The racing was the best ever on their particular track, and, the drivers and cars, were second to none.

In our area, it was ASCOT! The black clay was the best in the nation. Bubby and Dean put on the greatest shows in the history of racing. Of course, it is gone, and that makes this legendary track even more of a classic. Nothing could possibly compare to racing at ASCOT.

Of course, if you were from the Bay area, it was Baylands that got all of the attention. If you were from Sacramento, West Capitol was the greatest race track of them all. I find it interesting, that the best of the best, came from so many areas of our state. This, along with other regions of the country, has left us with quite a few legendary tracks. All of these tracks, of course, were the greatest of all time. They say that beauty is in the eye of the beholder. This is so true, especially, when the discussion of legendary tracks come up.

SPRINTS ON SPEED

Without a doubt, the World of Outlaws still rule the Sprint Car kingdom!

The new series of races, being telecast on SPEED Channel, really tells the story of the state of Sprint Car racing, in today's world. They have really put together a terrific package for the viewer.

In my view, a sports broadcast is only as good as the crew doing the reporting. In this case, the crew is exceptional to say the least. Bobby Gerould is the announcer. He goes way back with the Outlaws, and I have listened to him many times in northern California at Chico and other tracks.

The color man is Brad Doty, a former World of Outlaws driver. His input on driving styles is quite astute. Brad really gives you insight as to what is going on. Last, but not least, was someone new in the infield, doing driver and crew interviews. The smiling face of Sean Buckley was a pleasant surprise. He did an outstanding job with pertinent questions that were timely and informative. He also has a web site that is quite a riot to look at.

One can tell that this threesome love the sport. Their enthusiasm really comes out and makes for a great telecast. Tune in next time. I think you will enjoy the action.

2 LEAGUES

I am not a big NASCAR fan, but, I do like to observe the phenomenon created by this organization. NASCAR has become the giant industry that it is today, by either sheer luck, or very creative marketing. I am not quite sure, which avenue, brought it to the great heights it enjoys, over other forms of motor sports. Probably a little of both. Regardless, it is here to stay, like it or not!

One way for NASCAR to grow their sport, would be to create two leagues.

An Eastern and Western division that would run on the same weekends, but in different areas of the country. Just think of it, twice as many races, with a giant playoff at the end of the season. This would enable more tracks to hold NASCAR events, with most of the tracks having two events per year. What a windfall this would create, in an already successful league. Even the Las Vegas bookmakers would be thrilled, what with the expanded betting options, for their clientele.

This idea probably won't come to pass, but it is an interesting concept.

GOOD, BETTER, AND BEST

A lot of discussions center around which type of racing is the most exciting and fun to watch. Jim Naylor and I have had several rounds about this very subject, with neither of us budging, from our strong opinions on the subject. Therefore, I would like to extend my humble opinion, on my views of racing in its current forms.

GOOD: Formula One, NASCAR, IRL, and Champ Cars fill this category. A lot of follow-the-leader racing with little or no passing. Winning often depends on fuel and pit stop planning, and in NASCARs case, debris. Okay, but good just doesn't cut it for me.

BETTER: Winged Sprint Car Racing. I know a lot of folks from our area, think it is not exciting. However, I have been to many Winged Warrior Shows that have left the crowd breathless. It is true that the percentage of great shows is not as high as non-winged events. This situation is being addressed by the sanctioning bodies, and with a reduction in wing sizes coming, even better racing will result.

BEST: Traditional or Non-Wing Sprint Cars and Midgets. Hands down, the best of the entire menu offered by Motor Sports today. Especially here at Ventura Raceway. Our drivers put on a show that would be the envy of any track in the nation. Week in and week out, we are blessed with the best of the best.

THE "BIGS"

It is Sunday afternoon, Knoxville, Iowa. The sun is beating down at 90 degrees with 90% humidity . . . perfect midwest weather for the annual Knoxville Nationals. Fans are gathering for the "Big One" once again. This is what it is all about, the one race that every driver wants on his résumé.

Standing in front of the Hall of Fame, watching the big rigs rumble into town is an awesome sight. Here they come: Kinser, Saldana, Schatz, McCarl, Lasoski, The Wild Child. Their giant rigs with giant graphics depicting the car and driver have arrived. Each of these drivers, along with a hundred more, have one goal on their minds. Winning the most coveted Sprint Car race there is, the Knoxville Nationals!

I know that many think winged racing is not as good as the traditional style we see here in Southern California. This may be true. However, the Big Money, the Big Names, the Big News is all about the Outlaws. This traveling band of daring men,and brutally powerful racing machines has put Sprint Car racing on the map. Last place at the Nationals pay $7,000 . . . this is $5,000 more than first place at most major USAC races. It all boils down to one thing . . . marketing. The Outlaws, like them or not, have marketed themselves to the public, and the public has bought it. The Nationals are an event, not just another race.

MEMORIES

I was driving through Saugus the other day, and happened to pass the old Saugus Speedway. It still stands, even though time has passed it by. Today it is used as a swap meet. The surrounding area is packed with new shopping centers and industrial office complexes. I guess it is called progress, however, I am not so sure it has been for the best.

Saugus, along with Ascot, Gardena, the Carpenteria Thunderbowl, Oxnard Speedway, and others, have gone on to being only memories by most of our generation. The young folks of today never saw them, nor attended any racing at these old facilities. These memories will pass on to oblivion when our generation departs this earth. Today, any stadium built will be state-of-the-art in design, featuring the latest in technology. Of course, with the massive population growth of Southern California, chances of anything new are slim and none. By the way, slim left town!

We are very fortunate to have Ventura Raceway. The last of the Mohicans for racing venues in the greater southern California region. It is a throwback to another era. Quaint? Yes. Rustic? Yes . . . I wouldn't have it any other way. There is something about it that brings us back, to a simpler time, a simpler life.

BEST OF BREED

I had the pleasure of visiting the Peterson Museum this week and took in the Ferrari display. This is the 60th anniversary of the Ferrari Motor Cars. Needless to say, it brought back memories of the Santa Barbara Road Races. On display was a 1957 Testa Rosa driven by John Von Neuman, Ritchie Ginther, and Ken Miles. Ken Miles won with this car in 1962, and I was there to see it happen. There was also a 1967 Ferrari 275 GTB/4. My neighbor at the time, had one, and I got to go for a ride. We reached 140 mph, on Olives Park Drive. Quite a thrill to say the least! Today, Ferrari dominates Formula One with state-of-the-art technology and a huge budget.

They are truly the best of breed, recognized world-wide for their excellence.

Being the best in breed is something we all should strive for in both our personal, and business life. Tough to achieve, but worth the effort for the satisfaction it can bring. Our Thunderhead "Rising Star" award is now underway with six excellent drivers being chosen. Each of these drivers will be trying to be the "Best of Breed" and garner your vote, in the coming weeks. Stop by the Thunderhead booth and pick up a ballot. The race is on!

BIG DAY

WOW! It is Wags time again! Time flies when you are having a good time. This season has flown by like a rocket, and there are only a few weeks left to enjoy great racing. The Wags Dash is my favorite Ventura Raceway event. The Dash brings everybody out for a chance to socialize and enjoy each other's company. This year will be no different, what with Mrs. Wags Chili Feed, the Best Looking Driver Contest, and the Wheel Changing Contest highlighting the afternoon. This event is a major undertaking on the part of the Wag's group and has become the highlight of the season. A big "THANK YOU" to all of them for their efforts and support of Sprint Car racing at out track. Linda and I have hired a band to perform for this event. We hope you enjoy their music, as it is our thank you, to all the fans and drivers, at Ventura Raceway, for your support.

In addition to all of the above, we would like to give a big Ventura Raceway welcome to Mr. Tom Schmeh. Tom is the director of the National Sprint Car Hall of Fame and will be here with us to enjoy this big day. Each of us, as fans, should be a member of this great organization. The Hall of Fame, located in Knoxville, Iowa, is a must-see destination for any Sprint Car/Midget fan. Look up their web site at: www.sprintcarhof.com. Tom will be presenting Jim Naylor with the Hall of Fame, "Promoter of the Year" award. This is a well deserved award. Jim has done an exceptional job, in bringing Sprint Car racing back to southern California. Have a fun day!

STARS

Last week, I ventured north to meet up with some friends at the Tulare Thunderbowl, for a World of Outlaws show. As always, it is great fun to see, and be with fellow Sprint Car fans, that I see only a few times each year. These friendships are what it is all about. There is that common love of racing that we share and enjoy with each other on these occasions. Next up will be the Oval Nationals, which is always a blast.

Observing the packed crowd, which showed up to see the show, reveals how much "Star Power" plays in this sport. All of the big names were there. Kinser, Dolanski, Schatz, Saldana, Keading, Lasoski, The Wild Child, and many more. These are the traveling stars that the local fans only get to see once a year. That is the factor that makes it a not-miss event for the locals. Is the racing any better than their regular show, or for that matter, our regular show? Not really! Our regular show, is by far, a better pure racing event than most other races I have attended.

We have our own stars that race each week, and, we sometimes take them for granted.

Think back over this season, which is almost over, and you will recall some amazing duels for the checker. Every week has seemed to top the previous show in excitement and daring driver skills. Thank you to all of the drivers and crews that help make our events second to none.

THE PRELIM'S

I attended the Oval Nationals this past weekend at Perris. I guess you can call it the ultimate guy's trip. Three days of golf, horse racing and Sprint Cars all wrapped into one great time. It has become an annual trek for myself, and a few friends from northern California.

As usual, the best racing can be viewed on the preliminary qualifying nights. This seems to be true at all of the multi-night events I have attended. The Chili Bowl, the Knoxville Nationals, the Copper on Dirt, the Gold Cup, all share this single fact. Fans that miss out on these nights, really miss the best racing. Attendance on the prelim nights is always much less than the final night. This results in those fans missing out on the best of the show. The Prelim's at this years event were outstanding, probably, the best racing I have seen at Perris.

The Oval's have become one of the really big races of the year. Let's hope that they continue this event in the years to come. Seeing the "Best of the Best," from all over the country, makes for a great show. Sprint Car racing needs this type of event, if it is to grow in the future. If you do decide to attend the Oval's, or any other multi night show, be there for the whole deal.

Don't miss out on the best part, the Prelim's.

Ventura Raceway Articles

2008

Dr. Thunderhead

BACK AGAIN

Welcome back for another season of great action at the "Best Little Dirt Track" in America. It is truly a very unique place and is known all over the country as a great race place. In my travels to the Chili Bowl, and the Copper on Dirt, I constantly heard good things about the racing at Ventura Raceway. The fans that hadn't been here really wanted to visit us in the future. That really says something about the quality of this venue.

If you missed the Awards Banquet, we awarded the Thunderhead Rising Star Award, to Jonathon Henry. As usual, the voting was very close this year, as it always seems to be. We would like to give a special thank you to Dan Miller who outbid everyone for the Rising Star signature cap. His bid of $300 was very generous. This, along with the $200 in fan donations brought the total money award to $500. Jonathan will certainly need it, as he will be running his own car this season. We are also awarding him a right rear tire to start the season. We wish him the very best for this coming season as the Thunderhead "Rising Star" for 2007.

We look forward to again having the Rising Star contest for the 2008 season.

This year will feature a special 10 lap race in September for the contestants. With Thunderhead posting a $500 prize fund and others donating additional money, it should be a good one. I will keep you posted on the progress of this event. Meanwhile, sit back, relax, and LET'S GO RACING!

"DANCE WITH THE ONE THAT BROUGHT YOU"

Some have called it the biggest story in motor racing history. Others have questioned the ability, of it truly making a difference. Whichever camp you are in, the split of open wheel divisions CART (Champ Car) and IRL have finally buried the hatchet and merged.

This 13 year battle of ego's truly devastated the sport to the point of near oblivion. Tony George had all the cards in his favor. He just waited for Champ Car to go bankrupt, which it was on the verge of, just prior to the reconciliation. His victory, however, is a hollow one. Egos are a strange thing, in his case, he had a pocket book to match.

Being in sales most of my life, I long ago realized, that getting a new customer is easier, than getting back one you have lost. Just ask Ford, General Motors, and Chrysler. They failed to cater to their client base throughout the '70s and '80s and lost a large market share to Japanese and German manufacturers. Open wheel racing, with its split format, did the very same thing. They now face a major task in wooing back fans who have gone on to watch NASCAR. This is not easy, and I for one, feel that it will never be what it once was. The old saying, "dance with the one that brought you" sums it all up.

THE BIG DEAL

I watched part of the Bristol Cup race just to see if I was missing something.

Alas, not much to miss, as the endless stream of cars going around and around, pretty much puts me to sleep. However, the massive amount of fans filling this gigantic bowl was quite impressive. I can see how people get caught up in the circus atmosphere surrounding an event of this stature. The smaller venue only adds to this phenomenon. Most likely, there are a large group of fans who wish it had never grown to being such a monster-sized event.

The same can be said of the Chili Bowl. Over the last five years, it has grown to be the biggest event in open wheel racing. Many fans are complaining that it has lost its original small town atmosphere. The old atmosphere was more like a reunion of old friends, gathering each year to hang out, and have fun. Today, the event has changed.

And guess what? It will never be the same as it was in the "Good Old Days." It will just be different. Much like everything else in life. Your kids, and grandchildren, will never experience the lifestyle that you did. However, it will be the only experience they know. Someday, it will be their, "Good Old Days."

LOST THEIR CRUTCH

What happened to the "World's Greatest Drivers" at the Formula One Grand Prix of Australia? The powers that be removed traction control, and electronic engine braking, from the cars for this season. This resulted in a giant crash fest in both practice and the race.

So much for their boast, that Formula One, has the world's greatest drivers. However, it could have a good effect on the racing. Drivers, actually driving the cars, without a computer doing most of the work. What a concept!

I have a suggestion for them. Bring them all over to Ventura Raceway, and let them drive Sprint Cars for a change. Maybe even attend Kory's Driving School. They would learn in a hurry the art of sliding a car through the corners. This probably won't happen, as our racetrack could never hold the huge egos of this group. There is just not enough room here for them.

Nonetheless, it should make for better racing, and that could be a good thing. It might even make it worthwhile, to actually watch a race, rather than the results on Speed. Meanwhile, sit back and watch, some really great drivers, right here at Ventura Raceway. Each week, I am just amazed, at the talent that performs their driving skills for us.

THEY'RE BACK

I love the Midgets! Especially the full out, no-holds-barred version, that USAC brings to town each season. They put on a great show, and are truly made for this track. I only wish that we saw them more often. The USAC Midget division, is the only racing division left, featuring a variety of engine options. This, along with many chassis options, creates the one and only class, that leaves creativity, as a major component. They are a throwback to the old days, when each car was an individual project. Not completely, but close enough, to make them more interesting, than other forms of racing.

The problem facing this division, is the skyrocketing cost of building a car. This, along with the high cost of traveling their multi-state circuit, makes for smaller fields, as only the well-heeled need apply. Regardless, let's hope that they are around for a long time.

Welcome back USAC Midgets. It is always a pleasure watching you perform.

PARALLEL WORLDS

I had the pleasure of attending the horse races at Santa Anita this past Sunday. It was a great afternoon. There is something about just hanging out at the track, that is very relaxing and stress free. I have that same feeling when I am at the Sprint Car races. The one thought that came to my mind was horse racing and Sprint Car racing, are very similar. It is as though they run in parallel worlds.

Jockey's and Sprint Car drivers have a must-win attitude. They don't get paid for losing, and 2nd place is the first loser. This creates a must-win attitude, that makes for great racing action, in both sports. The best jockeys get the best horses, and it is the same in Sprint Car racing. The car owners want a winner in the seat, just as a horse owner wants a winner in the saddle. The result is the same for both sports. It rewards the fan with some terrific racing to watch and enjoy.

The other parallel situation, is actually a sad one. The crowds in both sports are aging rapidly. Young people have not been attracted to either sport for quite a while. This is a shame. The futures of both sports are in jeopardy of disappearing. Our junior programs are a step in the right direction. However, something needs to be done, to attract young race fans, to both sports. Let's hope something happens soon.

PARALLEL WORLDS (PART 2)

A few weeks ago I wrote about the parallel world that exists between Sprint Car racing and horse racing. Another parallel world exists between Sprint Car racing and the little known music niche of Americana/Folk/Blues music.

The music world is dominated by big business, dictating what is played and heard, by the general public. Yet, beneath the radar, exist some of the most creative music people in the industry. Unless you know about them, and seek them out, you will never know they exist. No big promotions and giant world tours exist for this group. It is a sad state of affairs for these very talented artists. Some of my favorites, to name a few, include: Jr. Brown, Split Lip Rayfield, Jimmie Dale Gilmore, Monster's of the Accordian, and Sista Monica.

The Sprint Car world shares a common bond with this group. These very talented drivers do their thing, mostly, for the love of the sport. They, like their musical brethren, enjoy little, if any, national exposure, or the big money that goes with the territory. It is as though these drivers, and us, the fans, belong to a secret society. We are the spoiled ones! It is time to let the secret out. Bring a friend or neighbor next week and introduce them to this great sport.

Let's not keep it a secret any longer, the sport needs your support.

WHO'S THE GREATEST

National Speed Sport News will be presenting a special section celebrating the 75th anniversary of the first Midget race, which was held in Sacramento, on June 4, 1933. They are asking for their readers help to answer the question: Who is the best Midget Car racer they have ever watched, and why?

My first thought was of Rich Vogler. His driving style, and fearless approach to racing, made him a legend. Billy Boat, was another great Midget driver, who dominated the sport while driving for John Larson. Over time, we have witnessed many of the great drivers who happened to drive Midgets. However, they also ran other forms of racing, and were not pure Midget drivers only.

Just one name comes to mind, when thinking of a pure, Midget-only driver. That name is Sleepy Tripp. Sleepy has to be the one and only, "Greatest Midget Driver Ever." Over 250 career feature wins, 104 USAC Western States feature wins, seven time Western USAC Midget Champion, 33 feature wins at Ascot. In addition, he was the 1974 USRC "Rookie" and Champion, the 1975 USAC "Rookie" and Champion, the 1976 USAC National Champion. No driver comes close to his accomplishments in the Midget field.

Sleepy was a true international star, having raced in Australia, New Zealand, and the United States. He gets my vote, how about you?...Let me know your thoughts.

INDY 500

"THE MONTH OF MAY"—I remember when it was the biggest month of the year, culminating, in the running of the "BIG ONE," at the Indianapolis Motor Speedway, on Memorial Day. The whole racing world tuned in to hear it on the radio. Later, TV and closed circuit broadcasts were the thing to see. An actual visit to see it in person, was the dream trip of a lifetime for any true race fan. I know it took me many years to finally make the journey to Indy, and it was a great trip.

Alas, times changed, and the luster was lost on this once great event. Greed and ego prevailed until it was almost reduced to just another race. Well, it is back, with a merger of the two warring factions, having finally buried the hatchet. This year's event has 39 cars entered and maybe, just maybe, bump day will mean something again. Let's hope so, because open wheel racing needs this premier event to be more than just another race.

One other aspect of this event, that will help, is the female drivers entered in the race. Three women will be competing against the men, and this will bring new fans to watch, and maybe become race fans in the process. Two of these women are legitimate racers, those being Danica Patrick and Sarah Fisher. The other woman, Milka Duno, is obviously the daughter or friend of someone with more money than common sense. She is a hazard on the track wherever she races and should not be allowed to compete at this level. Oh well, I guess one thing never changes...money talks, wherever you may be.

THE NEW 40s

It seems that when I was growing up, people in their 60s and older, were considered old timers. In reality, they were based on the lifestyle of that era. Today, things have changed for the better. People are living longer and for the most part, are active far past "retirement age."

You only have to look at our Senior Sprint Car Division to believe that old age is only a number. Ron Butler and John Richards are prime examples of living life to the fullest, no matter the age. Well into their 70s, they are still showing great driving skills. I am just amazed at their performance level every time they take the track.

Being a fan of old country music, I was able to see Porter Wagner perform at age 84. I am going to soon see a true legend, "Little Jimmy Dickens," who is now 87 and going on tour this month. His career dates back to the 40s, and he has worked his act for almost 60 years.

I guess that makes the 70s and 80s, the new 40s. The secret to it all is chasing your dreams and passions until time runs out. Give it a try! It is never too late change your life.

THE BEST OF THE BEST

National Speed Sport News had a feature on the 75 years of Midget racing in their last issue.

I had been looking forward to it, as the Midgets are the longest running group of race cars in existence. They are also my favorite form of racing. The diversity of the Midget division is what makes it so interesting.

I am sad to report, that *National Speed Sport News*, did not give the division their due respect. The issue, featured a lot of personal opinions, and a reader survey, that really didn't reflect the truth. I can't disagree with their choice, for the best-of-all-time, being Mel Kenyon.

However, a close second would have to be Sleepy Tripp. His record, which consisted of only Midgets, not other forms of racing, was incredible, for a guy from the west coast. He traveled east, and won two USAC national Midget titles. This, along with his dominance of the west coast, certainly should have been recognized. We, of course, are also to blame!

How many of us wrote in to voice our opinion?

In addition, USAC was not recognized for the major roll they have contributed the sport's longevity. Maybe the fact that they didn't run an advertisment, in the section, was the reason, for this obvious oversight. I thought they were going to be doing a lot of public relations to make the potential fans more aware of their product. Oh well, some things just never change.

PROMOTING THE FUTURE BY PRESERVING THE PAST

As I prepare to embark on my annual trip to the Knoxville Nationals, some thoughts come to mind. The slogan for the National Sprint Car Hall of Fame in Knoxville, Iowa is the title of this article. It is the goal of this organization, and everything they do, reflects this goal. I had a dream a while back, about doing a similar venture, right here in Ventura. I even went so far as to look for a location, and found the perfect spot. The only thing that holds up this dream is, of course, money . . . lots of it!

The history of racing in California is a rich one. The 75th anniversary of Midget racing just took place, with the first Midget race ever, occurring in California. Just think for a minute, about all of the race tracks, drivers, mechanics, car builders and promoters, that contributed to the great sport of racing, over the past 75 years. The more time that passes, leaves their legacy in serious doubt, of being remembered by generations to come. This is a great tragedy that should not be allowed to happen. Somehow, soon, an effort is needed to make this dream a reality before it is too late.

Speaking of reality, we have the Wagsdash Golf Tournament scheduled for September 5th. A lot of work will go into making this a fun event for drivers and fans of Ventura Raceway. Please get your entry forms in now, so we can make this a day to remember.

KING FOR A DAY

I just returned from the Knoxville Nationals. Eight nights of Sprint Car racing on big half-miles at Knoxville and Oscaloosa, Iowa. These are the major events in racing for Sprint Cars, with Knoxville having a purse of $1,000,000, for the four nights of the Nationals. Oscaloosa pays big money as well with a $30,000 to win non-wing show won by Dave Darland. Along with this, they have a front row challenge with $50,000 going to the pole winner if he goes to the back and wins the race. Joey Saldana gave it a shot, but was unable to make it happen. It only happened once, and I was there to see Jac Haudenschild pull off a miracle, to win the $50,000. The week is one big social event, with race fans and drivers from Australia, Canada, New Zealand and the U.S., meeting in this small town in Iowa. You have to be there to appreciate it.

The driver with the most wins is Steve Kinser, with 12 wins going back to 1980. More than any other driver in the history of the event, which goes back 48 years. That is why he is called the KING. Any other driver who wins this event is just a pretender to the throne. However, Donny Schatz has now won it three years in a row, and is presently the one to beat in this form of Sprint Car racing. It is interesting that when Donny won his first event three years ago, the crowd went wild and Kinser was booed by about half of the fans. After three years, Schatz is now drawing the boo's and Kinser has returned to exalted status in the eyes of the fans. It is interesting, how the fans build heroes, and then knock them off the pedestal once they reach the top. I have never been able to figure the reasoning behind this phenomenon. Does it apply to Ventura Raceway fans? Give it some thought.

WAGSDASH

He's back again! ... Ken Wagner and gang, a group of true Sprint Car fans, doing so much for the sport we all love. The Wagsdash is our big event of the year, bringing together a gathering of fans and drivers, for an afternoon and evening of fun and great racing. This event culminates a year of hard work and fundraising on the part of the Wags group. The dash provides a stage for drivers, who for whatever reason, have had a tough go of it during the season. These drivers get a chance to pick up some much needed money, for their low-budget race teams. Our own VRA 360 drivers also get a shot at this money. Kevin Kierce, earned his way in with the hard charger award in last weeks main event. Kevin charged from last place, to a fourth place finish, in what was a very exciting performance to watch. We wish him well in the Wagsdash tonight.

In addition to all of the festivities today, we have started an event, that we hope will become a Wagsdash tradition. By the time you read this, the first annual Wagsdash Golf Classic will have been completed. This event is also a fundraiser for both the Wagsdash and Ventura Raceway. Funds raised will go to the racers in the Wagsdash, and towards making some improvements to the fairgrounds, that house Ventura Raceway. This event is sponsored by the Committee to Support Ventura Raceway, a group of fans dedicated to improving the sport of racing at our facility.

LOVE-HATE RELATIONSHIPS

I have been thinking about all of the controversy between the various factions of Sprint Car racing. When compared to other forms of sports in this country and around the world, our numbers are quite small. Just consider the number of fans that follow football, basketball, and baseball. This, coupled with the NASCAR crowd, Formula One, and others, make our numbers small by comparison. We are a small, but loyal group.

But, are we truly loyal? Within our small numbers, we are split even further with the division of wing verses non-wing (traditional) styles of racing. In both divisions, we are further split between 305s, 360s and 410s, and some other various forms of the sport around the country. The wing fans are split big-time between the 360s and the 410s. 410 fans won't, for the most part, even attend a 360 show. I am always amazed at Knoxville, with the small crowd on Sunday night, for the 360 National Invitational. The fans are camped out a few blocks away, but they just don't attend. Monday night, the stands are packed to watch the 410s, so go figure, it just doesn't make sense.

Football is football; they don't have a separate group playing with 15 players, or a separate league of players weighing less than 200 pounds. It is just football! Maybe someday, the Sprint Car world will come to their senses and have one standard nationwide. It certainly would make sense, both from an economic and fan standpoint.

Race teams, would be able to race anywhere, at any time. This would make the sport more fan friendly and universal in appeal.

STILL A THRILL

Sitting in turn four at the Oval Nationals, I am reminded of my first Sprint Car race. It was many years ago at Ascot, and I was fortunate enough to see Parnelli Jones, Mario Andretti, and A.J. Foyt duel it out in the Trophy Dash.

The sight of Sprint Cars roaring down toward the corner was the most thrilling sports scene I had ever seen.

Nothing has really changed in all these years. The sound, the smell, and the sheer adrenalin rush is still the same. Watching the start of a Sprint Car main event, with twenty-four screaming sprinters heading into turns three and four, is truly the greatest spectacle in sports.

That is why I sit in turn four whenever I get down to Perris to watch the races.

Reserved seats in the main grandstand, forget it. I want to see the best action on the track, and it all occurs in the corners. Turn one at Ventura, turn four at Perris,

That is the place to be. Try it, I guarantee you will never sit anywhere else again.

Ventura Raceway Articles

2009

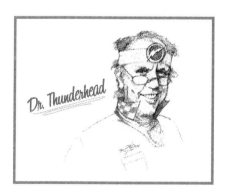

I'M BACK IN THE SADDLE AGAIN

If you are fortunate enough to have satellite radio, you can catch the Cowboy Music program on the weekend. The show features old-time Cowboy Music from the '40s and '50s. Gene Autry, Roy Rogers and other singers from that era are featured. Gene Autry's famous song, "I'm Back in the Saddle Again," reminded me, that we will be doing just that, as we return to Ventura Raceway for the start of the 2009 season. Racing at Ventura Raceway goes back a long way, and like the music of the cowboys, it just gets better with age. "I'm back in the saddle again, back where a friend is a friend," are part of the lyrics of this song. The lyrics fit the scene here at the Raceway. Friends, meeting up again, to share their love of our great sport, for another season of racing action.

If you missed the Awards Banquet, we awarded the Thunderhead Rising Star Award to Guy Woodward. As usual, the voting was very close this year, as it always seems to be. We would like to give a special thank you to Kevin Kierce and Bruce Douglas, who both bought a "Rising Star" signature cap, with donations of $100 each. In addition, super fan Richard Baker, also donated $100. These generous donations brought the money fund up to $600. This money will help Guy towards a successful 2009 season. We wish him the very best for this coming season as the Thunderhead "Rising Star" for 2008. We look forward to again having the Rising Star contest for the 2009 season. Look for our list of drivers to be announced in May. Now, sit back in the saddle, for a great night of racing.

THE JOURNEY

There is a famous quote I read once, "Destination is merely a by-product of the journey."

This is certainly a true statement that I try and live by. My most recent example of this, would be my annual journey to the Chili Bowl. I drive there, instead of taking a plane, for the very reason stated in the quote. When one flies, one only see's two airports and a rental car stand. Driving enables one to really see the country, and experience first hand the many interesting people, and places, that make up this great land of ours.

Finding a decent meal is an important part of the journey. I have been a fan of the Food Channel show, *Drive-ins, Diners & Dives*, which features unique places to eat around the country. I try and follow this concept on my trip and have found some great places along the way. In Tonapah, Arizona, there is the Tonapah Family Restaurant which features great home cooking. In Dragoon, Arizona is a truck stop which features an attraction featuring "THE THING." This is a must-stop, and for a buck, you get to see it.

The Rancher's Grill in Deming, New Mexico, features the world's best Country Fried Steak. Rule number one is "Never eat in a chain restaurant." Get off the highway and experience the really unique establishments.

Oh yes, the Chili Bowl . . . It was great as usual: big crowd, big car count, lots of fun with friends from around the world. However, it was just the destination, not the journey.

THE GOOD OLD DAYS

I was sitting in the grandstands at the Tulare Thunderbowl last Friday night with two of my racing friends from Northern California. We hadn't seen each other in a while, and, it was good to get together for the World of Outlaws event.

We have enjoyed these events together for many years, and talk turned to how it used to be. Back in the day, Brent Kaeding could challenge the travelers. Those days are gone, and will never return. Drivers like Stevie Smith, Andy Hillenberg, along with Steve Kinser, Sammy Swindell and others would thrill the crowd with their driving skills. Steve and Sammy are still going, but something seemed to be missing for us. Maybe it's the evolution of the cars. Today they are all the same, making for racing that is not as exciting as it used to be. In those times, Karl Kinser was the difference between Steve and the rest of the field. It was more about set up, and reading the track, than it is today. Today, it is pedal to the metal, and the quality of racing at this top level is just not as good as it once was. However, Tulare is a small town, and the Outlaws only appear once or twice a year. This makes it a big deal in this area, and the crowd loves it. This event, is at a special place, and a special night, for all to enjoy. We did just that, as the evening ended all too soon, and it was time to go back home.

We happen to be blessed with great racing action week after week. We are truly spoiled, with the great venue, and racing action, at Ventura Raceway. The Good Old Days may be gone for us, however, for the younger crowd, these will be their Good Old Days. Enjoy them, as time changes everything.

MIDGET MADNESS

The Midgets are back for another great show at Ventura Raceway. Just look back at the great history, that has evolved over the past 75 years. What other form of motor sports can come close to Midgets? They have seen boom and bust times, but somehow have survived to this day. They were the King of Motor Sports after World War II at places like Gilmore Stadium and other venues. Crowds were huge and the sport flourished in the limelight. They have had their ups and downs over the years, but somehow manage to keep coming back.

Midget racing had another golden era during the 90s, when ESPN put them on the TV screen. We got to see many of the super stars of today battle it out right here at Ventura Raceway. This venue, along with the television coverage, turned them into NASCAR mega stars. Drivers such as Tony Stewart, Jeff Gordon, Jason Lefler and others owe their success to the "Best Little Dirt Track in America."

The Chili Bowl has helped revive the Midget Madness. Three hundred cars showed up for this years event. Every top driver in the country wants to win it, and hold the Golden Driller Trophy. Let's hope that our coming event in November draws a good field and becomes another "must-win" event. It has all of the potential to do just that.

Let the Madness continue!

TOP DOG

"THE MONTH OF MAY"—I remember when it was the biggest month of the year, culminating in the running of the "Big One" at the Indianapolis Motor Speedway, on Memorial Day. I couldn't wait to hear it on the radio, with Sid Collins, calling the action in such a way, that I could picture in my mind, the actual event as it unfolded.

Then, a miracle of modern science was introduced, with closed circuit broadcasting of the race. There it was, in living "black and white" at a theater near you. Today, you can sit at home, and watch it unfold on you big screen TV.

That is not all that has changed! The Big One is no longer the Top Dog, and it has struggled to maintain some semblance of importance, in the racing world. The IRL race results are just a footnote under the ETC section in the sports page. The real change that has affected Indy Car racing, has been technology. Along with your state-of-the-art TV, the cars are now high tech Xerox copies of each other. Each team entered has to spend millions just to be competitive. Gone are the days of individual ideas and creative concepts, that would set your entry apart from the others. The Novi, The Turbine, and others, are a thing of the past, replaced with off-the-shelf cars, and "Pay to Race" drivers.

The Big One will be back this month, and, yes, I will watch it again. I also go to the Turkey Night Grand Prix. This is another example of technology ruining a great event.

Oh well, at least we still have Midgets and Sprint Cars, on the dirt, here at Ventura Raceway. It doesn't get any better than this.

RAIL BIRD

If you caught the Kentucky Derby last Saturday, you were treated to another great upset by an underdog. Mine That Bird, ridden by Calvin Borel, rode the rail all the way around, and shocked the crowd with a come-from-behind victory. The horse paid $103.20 to win, the second highest payoff in Derby history. The jockey and horse thundered down the stretch past million dollar horses. The horse was originally purchased for $9,500 and had not raced in seven months. The trainer towed Mine That Bird, in a trailer behind his pick-up, all the way from New Mexico, a trip that took 21 hours of drive time. They stood together in victory, the jockey in tears and the trainer, Bennie Wooley Jr., holding court in an emotional win.

What does this have to do with Sprint Car racing, you ask? It brought back fond memories of Brandon Thompson, winning the big race last season, for $5,000. His victory was of the same magnitude. Old car, old trailer, underdog driver, with talent and guts to stick to his plan. A rail run to victory, celebrated by Grandpa, Dad and Brandon in an emotional victory circle. These moments should be cherished by all of us, as this is what it is all about. Live life at full speed, you never know where it will take you.

BREAK TIME

The Ventura County Fair is here. It is time for our summer break from the regular race schedule. This break gives the race teams some time to rebuild, and get set for the run to the finish, and a possible championship, in their respective divisions.

I will be heading out to the Knoxville Nationals for their annual week-long event.

The Nationals pay the biggest purse in Sprint Car racing. Attendance is around 40,000 fans and racers for the week. It is truly a spectacle that features the best-of-the-best in Sprint Cars. This year, they will be featuring the non-wing cars on Sunday night the 9th of August. I am really looking forward to this night, as a lot of fans from the midwest, have never seen our style of racing. These fans are mostly the younger crowd who grew up with the wing cars as their only form to watch.

In addition, the trip allows me to visit the National Sprint Car Hall of Fame. The Hall sits right behind turn two and is a must-visit for any Sprint Car fan. They have just completed the second floor, which features the photos of all the inductees, along with a movie theater. All of this is possible because of Sprint Car fans support, which brings me to an important subject. As Sprint Car fans, all of us should be a member of this organization. You can join on their web site, which is sprintcarhof. com. Their motto is "Promoting the Future by Preserving the Past." Your support is needed to continue their mission.

HALL OF FAME

I have returned from my annual trip to the Knoxville Nationals. I have good news for Sprint Car fans. The Hall of Fame has completed a significant expansion of the second floor. It now includes all of the photos of the Hall of Fame inductees, and along with this, a state-of-the-art movie theater. It was quite interesting to watch the films of the glory days of Sprint Car racing. Mario, Parnelli, Jud Larson, and other greats, dueling it out over the dusty dirt tracks of their era. No roll cages, seat belts or other safety features that are commonplace today. Each of their cars are of a unique design, developed by various designers. Times have certainly changed, mostly for the better, where safety is concerned. The cookie-cutter aspect of car design in today's world, however, leaves something to be desired, when compared to the cars of that by-gone era.

As Sprint Car fans, we owe a debt to the work that the Hall of Fame is doing. I highly recommend that you visit this great place. You will find a showplace that lives up to their motto: "Promoting the Future, by Preserving the Past." Each of us needs to be a member of this great organization. I brought back with me applications for each of you to join. Stop by the Thunderhead booth tonight and pick one up.

Your support will help keep Sprint Car racing alive for the future.

SUPERFAN

I always enjoy reading Ron Hedger's column in *National Speed Sport News*.

Each year, he reports on the SuperFans, who attend the most races during the year.

The 2008 winner was Bob Schafer from Wisconsin who attended 273 races. This is an incredible feat, considering the cost of gas last year. He must be retired, as no person working full-time could possibly manage this feat. Of course, he is in the midwest, which is an advantage over anyone living on the west coast. In the midwest, racing is available many nights per week. Californian, Doug Brown, managed to get to 53 races. This is a lot, considering the fact that most races run on Saturday night in California.

I decided to tally up my races for 2008, and came up with 49 race nights for the year.

Of course, 25 were here at Ventura. Throw in the Chili Bowl, Manzy, Perris, Tulare, Santa Maria, Turkey Night, and Knoxville, and the total was 49 nights of racing. Just think of how many it could have been, if we had racing many nights, like they do in the Midwest.

So, how does your race total stack up? Let me know what your 2008 race total was, and I will award the winner, with one of our Thunderhead all-over design hats. In addition, you will have bragging rights, as the Thunderhead SuperFan, at Ventura Raceway.

A GOOD CAUSE

I have two good causes that I am working on and I need your support for both of them.

First, is the National Sprint Car Hall of Fame membership drive. I wrote about this last week and I have enclosed a membership application in the program for this week. As Sprint Car fans, we need to be members of this great organization. Membership is only $25 per year so fill out the form and drop it off to me tonight. If we get 20 members, I will have a drawing for a Thunderhead T-shirt among those joining. If we get 25 members, we will have a drawing for a National Sprint Car Hall of Fame sweatshirt.

Show your support and join tonight!

Second is the Kiwanis fundraiser, of which I am in charge. This event is Oct. 3rd and it is a poker run car/motorcycle rally. It starts at MB2 Raceway in Newbury Park at noon and finishes at Ventura Raceway for an evening of racing. Cost is only $50 per person and you get an event shirt, hot dog lunch, entry to Ventura Raceway and parking. The Foster Children's Program is a charity where the profits will go. This great program serves children in need throughout Ventura County. I would appreciate your support with your running in this event . . . it is for a good cause. A flyer sheet/entry form is enclosed in your program. Thanking you in advance . . . Tom

TWO-WIDE

I actually watched some of the NASCAR race last weekend, and noticed something new.

Two-wide restarts, after a yellow caution period, have been implemented. Considering how boring this form of racing can be, it was rather refreshing to see. At least they are trying to bring some excitement to a sport, that has turned into a long train of cars, that go round-and-round, in an endless parade. Great sound, a lot of colorful cars, however, not much goes on in the passing department. This, in addition to team racing, has made the NASCAR racing group about as exciting as watching paint dry.

There is nothing quite as exciting as the start of a Sprint Car race. Side-by-side, blasting down the front straight into turn one, is the ultimate sports action, that a fan can watch.

The only thing that really comes close is bull riding with an 8 second (maybe) ride.

I would like to see Sprint Cars adopt the side-by-side restart. I think it would bring about another dimension to an already thrilling exhibition of speed and daring. Choosing the inside or outside line, would be crucial in the driver's race strategy. This crucial decision would play a huge part in the race outcome, adding to an already thrilling spectacle. What are your thoughts? Let me know.

PAST AND PRESENT

I have written several times about the National Sprint Car Hall of Fame and the great job it does in "Preserving the Past while Promoting the Future" goals.

This month's bulletin from the Hall reflects news that the past is disappearing at a rapid rate. Walt James, a familiar figure here at Ventura Raceway has passed on at the age of 86. His energetic lifestyle, will surely be missed, as he gave it his all, in preserving the past right up to the end. Another great driver, Billy Wilkerson, also left us at age 82. Another gentleman, Palmer Berger, who I had the pleasure of meeting, and becoming friends with, at the Chili Bowl and the Knoxville Nationals, has also passed on. Palmer always had a big smile, and a hand shake, whenever we would run into each other at these events. I will miss him, as he was a wealth of information, on the who, what, when, where, and why of the racing world.

As to the present, we have all the young guns, vying for the Thunderhead "Rising Star" award. This year's group is part of the future of Sprint Car racing. The season is drawing to a close, so be sure and get your vote in for your choice in the contest.

The nominees are: Brian Camarillo (22c)—Tyler Edwards (41K)—Don Gansen (7G)—Cody Kershaw (27)—Justin Kierce (48T). Stop by the Thunderhead booth and place your vote.

WHAT HAPPENED?

The year was 1946 and the country was fixated on Midget Car racing. From the west coast to the east coast, huge crowds were filling race tracks to the maximum.

Not just on Saturday night, but four and five nights a week, the Midgets were the toast of the town. In California, there were two circuits, the red and the blue doing battle at such venues as the Coliseum, the Rose Bowl, Gilmore Stadium and many other venues. The Coliseum and the Rose Bowl are still part of Southern California. Midget Cars have long disappeared from those venues and the glory days of that era. However, we still have a loyal group of fans and drivers following this most exciting sport.

What happened to cause the demise of this great sport? The answer to that can be very complicated, and many theories prevail. One theory is as follows: This is a big country, and Midget Racing was fragmented on a regional basis. AAA, and many other groups sanctioned Midget Racing from coast to coast. Then, along came the National Football League, and Major League Baseball. They expanded coast to coast in the '50s and became the dominate sport for people to go and see. Had Midget Racing formed a national league with a world series type finish, perhaps it would still be a major league sport today. Alas, it is what it is! The Chili Bowl is now the World Series of Midget Racing. Perhaps the Fall Classic here at Ventura, will develop into an equally major league event, in the years to come. Let's hope so.

OUT OF SIGHT, OUT OF MIND

Race fans file into the speedway each Saturday night, looking forward to another night of great racing. The early arrivals stake out their preferred seats, and mark their territory for the evening's activities. Long-time race friends gather here to enjoy the evenings events. No problems, just sit back, and enjoy the events about to unfold before them. Yes, they're hooked. Race junkies, all of us, just can't get enough of this great sport.

Another group also checks in early, but with another mission in hand. The Scoring Committee. That small group of individuals, who keep track of the evenings events. Hidden away in the tower, out of sight, and out of mind.

This group of unsung heroes, keeps track of every car, in every race, week after week. This thankless job, goes unseen, by all of us fans in the stands.

Our only function is to have a great time, while they toil under endless stress to make sure the results are correct and the rules are followed. They deserve a standing ovation from us. Maybe, if time allows, we can do just that.

SPARKLE & TWANG

I visited the Autry National Center of the American West recently. They have an incredible display of memorabilia provided by Marty Stuart and his wife Connie Smith. These two are part of the history of country music, and have collected quite a collection of artifacts, from the early days of this music genre. Country music stars of the '40s, '50s and '60s were unique in both their musical and wardrobe styles. Lots of sparkle in their outfits, and lots of twang in their musical offerings, gave them a look and sound like no other.

Today, the country music stars are just Xerox copies of each other, with nothing unique to set them apart from each other.

In our sport, it is somewhat the same. The cars are Xerox copies, bought off the shelf, and basically all built to the same specs. The creativity, of individuals doing their own thing, is no longer an option. This may be okay, but I still miss seeing the unique designs, created by one's imagination, in a quest to outdo the other teams in the sport.

The Autry has done a terrific job in preserving history, and this current display is one you should not miss. It is too bad we don't have something like this on the west coast, to honor and remember the creative people and machines, that founded our great sport of auto racing.

RESPECT

I looked up the word respect in the dictionary, and it is defined as follows: The willingness to show consideration or appreciation. This was one of the concepts, that was drilled into us as children, by our parents. In today's world, there seems to be a lack of respect, by certain people, in positions that should reflect that concept. I am talking about the stunt pulled off by Kyle Busch. Smashing his guitar trophy like he was rock star at the Memphis Nationwide Series race. Rock stars have always been an angry bunch, thumbing their noses at society in more ways than one. There is no room for this behavior byr those involved in the racing game. They are looked up to by kids all over the world, and need to be respectful, of the image they portray. Down the road, Kyle will most likely regret his decision to burn this bridge.

We have all burnt bridges in our past, that we would like to be able to rebuild. The song, "Lost River," by the Nitty Gritty Dirt Band, is a prime example of this story. As I listen to this song, while writing this article, it reminds me of the many bridges I have burnt. The result of which, is mostly regret, at action taken in the heat of the moment. Let's hope that Kyle changes his outlook, as he may never be able to return to higher ground, after burning the bridge in Memphis.

Ventura Raceway Articles

2010

OUTLAWS

Tonight is the first of three All Coast Challenge races that are scheduled for this year. These events are quite unique as they have a $5,000 to win purse for each race, and $5,000 for total points of the three races. As usual, we will have the "outsiders" arriving to try and pick up the cash. The purse for these events is among the highest for Sprint Cars in the state. Therefore, we will see several drivers coming from outside our home area. It is like the "Outlaws," riding into town and trying to run off with the cash. I can't blame them, as money is tight these days for anyone trying to run a race team.

The "World of Outlaws" got their name from this very form of drivers, who traveled anywhere the money was good. Ted Johnson organized this merry band of renegades into the biggest Sprint Car group in the country. Like them, or not, they command the biggest purses of any group, and fans pay much more to attend their events.

I say welcome, to these outlaws, who are here to steal the show. Our regular guys are a tough crowd to beat, and it should make for a great show.

SIDE-BY-SIDE

Both NASCAR and the World of Outlaws have instituted a double file restart on yellow flag restarts this season. This ruling was started to create some excitement in the races, that have become follow-the-leader parades. NASCAR races, which are marathon events of hundreds of miles, at a high rate of speed, had become nothing more than sleep-inducing events. The World of Outlaws heat races, are usually over after turn two of the first lap. This is fine if you want to see cars running at very high speeds, however, I prefer an event that is contested from start to finish. Granted, there is nothing more exciting than the start of a race, as the cars scream into turn one and battle for position. In the event of a yellow flag, having a side-by-side restart gives an advantage to the driver who has been passed, and this is not a fair situation. We have seen several versions of restarts over the years: back stretch cone, front stretch cone, etc. The best method is still the traditional system used here at Ventura Raceway. Green flag the race coming out of turn four, single file, and let the drivers earn their positions. Sometimes, traditional rules and values are best.

WHAT IF?

The USAC Midgets return tonight for another thrilling duel of these mighty cars and drivers. Nothing compares to the action that is about to unfold in front of us, with this group that has been around for more than 75 years. The Midgets are the unsung heroes of dirt track racing.

What if they were combined with the USAC Sprint Cars, as a traveling group across the country? The World of Outlaws are just such a group, and command big purses and even bigger crowds. Their arrival in town creates an atmosphere that is electric. It is unfortunate that the USAC group is split between a national group and the western section. This situation leaves the western swing somewhere out in left field, and the total package is hurt by this situation.

It would be a bold move to combine the two and go for it! However, I think the time is right for just such a move. A true national tour would allow drivers to actually make a living at their sport. This would raise public awareness of USAC Midget and Sprint Car racing. What if? . . . Why not?

BLESSED

Looking back, it has been a great season of racing so far. We have been blessed with good weather and great racing. Of course, we are spoiled, when you compare our situation with that in the rest of the country. Just look to your right, and what do you see? Palm trees, the ocean, the pier. You can walk over and watch the surfers as they try and conquer the waves. There is nothing like it at any racetrack in the country.

All of this would not be possible, without the team of people, who show up every week and help out with the many duties needed to pull off our event. This group, of stalwart individuals, make it happen, so we can sit back and enjoy the sport of racing. We may not see them, as in the case of the Tech Inspection crew or the Scoring Committee. They go about their task each week, invisible to the crowd sitting in the grandstand. Our only function is to have a great time, while they toil under endless stress to make sure the program goes off without a hitch.

We are truly blessed, and I thank them all for the efforts, in keeping this great race place alive and well each season.

CHANGES

An old saying goes, Times They Are A-Changin'. I guess they really are when it comes to auto racing. I watched the finish of the Taladega race just to see how the finish would turn out. Go figure, there was the usual crash bang that resulted, from use of the new green, white, checker, with the cars starting two-wide. This change, two-wide and a finish under the green flag, was done to create some excitement in an otherwise boring event. If you consider wild crashes as the answer, then this change was good for you.

Another change is coming to the Indy 500. What was once the Month of May will now be a weekend devoted to trying to gather a crowd to watch the qualifying trials. Pole day will consist of a 90 minute shootout to earn a chance to run for the pole. The nine fastest cars will make a run for the pole. It gets complicated, and weather could be a big factor in how the show turns out. They will still have bump day, although, with car counts being what they are, that may not mean much. This change might be a good one, as the crowds, the last few years, have been dismal at best. I wish them the best and will watch with interest to see if it works.

Times change, and the biggest change is the cost of racing at the upper levels. The rising costs are a key reason you do not see more American drivers racing at Indy. We live in a world that is global and changing, so get used to it.

HOPE

Today they will run the Preakness Stakes in Baltimore, with 14 horses vying for the second leg of the Triple Crown. The Triple Crown is the ultimate goal for a thoroughbred horse owner. The last horse to win the Triple Crown was Affirmed in 1978. Horseracing needs another Triple Crown winner in their desperate attempt to revive, what once was the Sport of Kings. Jockey Calvin Borel will try and add this second leg of the series aboard Super Saver, the Kentucky Derby winner. Hope can be an empty thing, as time passes you by.

On Memorial Day, 33 drivers will try and win the Indy 500. This is another form of racing that is trying to revive itself, to its former days of glory. The Indy 500 was once the ultimate racing event in the world. Today, it is a sad affair featuring extreme modern technology, with little success, except for everyone wishing the good old days were still here. We still watch, hoping it might somehow return, pitting hope against hope.

These once towering entertainment events, are very similar to aging show business stars, still trying to capture the roar of the crowd. The El Portal Theater in North Hollywood is a venue that is featuring some of these aging relics. Debbie Reynolds, Joe Bologna, and my all-time favorite, Rip Taylor. Yes, I am going to see Rip in his one-man show next week. I still remember him at the lounge at the Sahara Hotel in Vegas back in the day, with his outrageous humor and flying confetti. You see, I still keep hoping, in spite of the odds, that the glory will somehow remain, even if it is just in my mind.

BIG TIME INDY

I always get a kick out of the letters to the editor of *National Speed Sport News*. Time and again, we read from fans wanting the Indy 500 to have more American drivers. We all wish it could be true, however, the truth is that times have changed for this event. The world has changed and Indy has changed with it.

Gone are the days when a Los Angeles car dealer could field an Indy car and offer a ride to a Parnelli or other great drivers. The cost of racing at this level is off the charts and only the very mega rich can truly play the game. Major sponsorship is the key for any driver if he wants to be part of the game. They must bring along a big dollar sponsorship in order to secure a ride. This, combined with two mega teams, Ganassi and Penske, leaves many a qualified driver on the outside looking in.

It is the same in other entertainment fields as well. The movie industry is now totally controlled by the major studios. Their blockbuster movies cost millions to produce and distribute. There is no room or financing for the small independent producer and his or her art film. This leaves some great actors, directors and others on the outside with literally no chance. It all boils down to money, and money talks or you walk. It is what it is, so all of us who yearn for the old days, might as well accept it, and just enjoy the show that is Indy.

4TH OF JULY

The 4th of July means the season is half over, and what a season it has been.

The racing in all of our divisions has been stellar. If the rest of the season is at all as good, then we will have a lot to be thankful for. Normally we are dark on this weekend, so it is kind of a treat to be here on the 4th.

One of the things, I am impressed with as I travel around, is the patriotic outlook of racing fans. The playing of the Star Spangled Banner is treated respectfully, and a loud cheer always follows its playing. The one thing that always drives me nuts is when a track will have a fan or local singer try and sing this most difficult song. At Oscaloosa, Iowa, they had an Elvis impersonator, who not only could not sing, but he forgot the words. The next night they had someone who couldn't carry a tune in a bucket. The song is one tough piece that requires a great vocal range that few singers possess.

It is always best to have a recorded version, unless you have a singer who is truly blessed with the vocal range needed. Knoxille has such a person in one of the local fans who has a pure voice. She sang the Star Spangled Banner, God Bless America, the Australian National Anthem and the Canadian National Anthem. Four songs in a row and she never missed a beat. The huge crowd goes wild when she is finished, showing their appreciation for a true talent, not some wannabe. Have a great 4th of July weekend.

LOOKING BACK

It seems as though the older one gets, the more things we have to look back on.

I bought my first car when I was fifteen years old. It was a 51 Chevy which I customized into a lead sled. My next car was a 53 Mercury which was simply a real hot looking car.

When I was a senior in high school I got the urge to have a Bug-Eye Sprite. This was during a time when sports cars were all the rage in Southern California. So, off I went to the dealer, and bought a brand new one. I even financed it with monthly payments of $35. Just try and finance a car today at age 17, not a chance.

Thus, began my experience with British cars, as I owned several over the next few years.

They included the original Bug-Eye, an MG Midget, another Bug-Eye, a Sunbeam Alpine, and last, but not least, a MGB in 1964. I was a member of the Tri-County Sports Car Club, and the El Conejo Sports Car Club. These were fun times, as we ran road rally's and did a lot of slalom racing over the decade of the sixties. The one major problem with British cars was the electrical systems. They were made by a company named Lucas, which also was the major manufacturer of refrigeration products in England. The joke was, 'Why do the British like warm beer? … Lucas.' However, we put up with all of the problems, as we were part of a special group of car owners, or so we thought, and waved to each other as we passed on the highway.

This was a unique time, and you can visit this era Sunday at the Channel Islands Harbor. The Central Coast British Car Show featuring Triumph will run from 9 a.m. to 3 p.m. I will be going, just to look back at a very special time in my life.

ENTERTAINMENT

Once again, we have the pleasure of seeing the USAC Midgets at our raceway.

Steeped in historic tradition, dating back to the mid 1930s, they have managed to maintain a loyal following. Both drivers and fans still love these little machines for both the action and beauty they bring to the table. There is nothing like them in any other form of auto racing.

However, they are becoming an endangered species! The cost of owning and racing one of these works of art has just gone off the charts. Few owners can today justify the cost of a $40,000 engine. This, along with purses that have not risen in decades, has chased away many teams from the competition. Based on the Chili Bowl, there are around 300 Midgets in this country. They all show up for that event, even though a large number of those only race the Chili Bowl and then return to the garage for another year.

Let's compare Midget racing with other forms of entertainment, and that is what it is, entertainment. You pay around $15 for any seat in the house, so compare that with a cheap seat at the Chumash Casino for a singer at $45. Go to a Laker game and you will need a bank loan to cover the cost of your seat. Yet, we somehow expect to see these great Midget shows, for the same cost as a movie ticket. Something makes me think we are all living in the past, yet, we will spend $7 for a beer that was 50¢ back in the day.

Times have changed, except for this form of entertainment. We now are faced with either Midget racing becoming extinct, or a cost reduction miracle in engine expense.

Let's hope something is done before it is too late.

BIG SHOW

Many years ago, Ed Sullivan would welcome the audience and say he had a "Really Big Show." It sounded more like a "Really Big Shoe" and it became kind of a trademark for him, which comedians would mimic in their acts.

Well, Jim Naylor has a "Really Big Show" scheduled for tonight and it is a "Shoe In" to be a good one. The All-Coast Challenge, sponsored by Big Mike and the All-Coast Construction Company will be the final leg of a three-race series that is gaining in stature each season. This year, we will be invaded by two of Sprint Car racing's stellar stars. Dave Darland and Jon Stanbrough, two of the top USAC stars from the national circuit will fly in to challenge our local guys. They will have their hands full, as our locals are a tough bunch, and should not be taken lightly.

Think back to when we first had Sprint Cars on this little track . . . They said it couldn't be done, but it became a reality, and is today, one of the top shows anywhere in the country. The future looks good for this series, and with the addition of a Midget Division next season, it can only be better. Thank you Mike, your support of this series is appreciated by both the fans and drivers.

So, sit back and get ready for a "Really Big Show"! . . . We've got the best-of-the-best, at the "Best Little Dirt Track in America."

LAST CHANCE

And you thought the season was over. Well, sit back and enjoy the best-of-the-best Midget drivers in the nation, right here at Ventura Raceway. This show should bring back memories of the famed Thursday Night Thunder series, hosted here at our raceway.

In addition, Thanksgiving week and the Midgets will return to the dirt, where they truly shine. Like they say, dirt is for racing and pavement is to get there.

This evenings show will also be the last chance to vote for your favorite Thunderhead "Rising Star" candidate. This seasons crop of drivers is probably the best we have seen in several years. They are as follows: David Bezio, Charlie Butcher, Don Gansen, Dakota Kershaw, Justin Kierce, Kenny Perkins and Brody Roa. Each of these young drivers has shown the ability and drive to be the winner of this award. Stop by the Thunderhead booth and vote for your favorite driver and also make a cash donation which will go to the winner.

I am also working with the National Sprint Car Hall of Fame on their annual fundraising program. They have a raffle for a Sprint Car with all of the money raised going to the Hall of Fame. Tickets are $20 or 6 for $100 and are available at our booth. This fundraising effort is a key part of keeping the sport of Sprint Car racing alive. Your donation will go towards a good cause and you might just win a state-of-the-art Sprint Car.

Ventura Raceway Articles

2011

ON THE ROAD AGAIN

Iconic singer/songwriter, country legend, Willie Nelson will turn 78 this month. A major concert in Texas will celebrate this event. It is not often that a person with his lifestyle manages to beat the odds and live to a ripe old age. A major concert is planned and I am sure that every country artist in Texas will perform. Willie still hits the road each year for over 100 appearances, which is quite a feat considering his age. His tour bus, Honeysuckle Rose, is his home on these journeys. If you have never been to a Willie Nelson concert, I suggest you do so. They are unique events and the talent he displays gives him a position at the top of all-time entertainers.

Willie's signature song, "On the Road Again" is the first song I play when I hit the road to travel to other race tracks in my tour bus—the "Thunder Van." Old Thunder will soon be pressing 200,000 miles, and like Willie, it keeps on performing like a true trooper. This song sets the tone for the adventure that lies ahead. Seeing old friends and making new ones is quite a treat. Throw in some good racing and it makes it all worth the effort.

The one thing that I have noticed in my travels recently is the lack of a program for the fans at every track I visited. Calistoga, Merced, Perris, Hanford, Tulare and Lemoore. Not one program at any venue. This reminds me of how great our weekly program is here at Ventura. A full color cover with stats and driver lists, along with articles and driver features. This is just another reminder of how much effort goes into making this weekly program the best anywhere. You just have to "hit the road" to realize it.

MIDGET MADNESS

Tonight starts what will probably be the beginning of a great tradition at Ventura Raceway. The first race of our new VRA Midget Division will take to the track for the "Battle at the Beach." Our drivers, will be challenged by the USAC Midget Division, in what should be a great event.

What will the future hold for this bold step by promoter Jim Naylor? The same question was asked when the Chili Bowl first ran twenty-five years ago. What were they thinking at the start of what has become the premier Midget race in the country? I predict that this series will develop into a very important facet of open wheel racing in this country. All of the pieces are in place for this much needed series. The future of Midget racing will surely be altered if it is a success. If the 2011 season ends with the big Midget race just prior to the Thanksgiving weekend, then it could develop into something that would be a really "Big Deal." That is what I am hoping for. A return of Midget racing to the status it held back in the old days, when Turkey Night was really something important, for a driver and the fans to be part of. Enjoy tonight, it is the start of something that just might become a tradition. Midget Madness rides again!

MIDGET MANIA

Welcome to the best Midget Car racing facility in the country. Last Saturday night, we were given a taste of what this series will bring to the sport. Brian Camarillo's run from back in the pack to finish second was a sight to behold. This is just the beginning of what I think will turn out to be some of the best racing you can find anywhere. Tonight they will be back in action for another thrilling event.

Ventura Raceway was part of the Midget Revival, when ESPN featured the Thursday Night Thunder, live from Ventura, and other tracks in the country. This was a series that should still be going on today. However, the cost of live TV went off the charts, and alas, it and Midget racing fell off the radar. The popularity of the Chili Bowl revived the interest in this form of racing. Now, Ventura Raceway, will once again be the catalyst in bringing this exciting form of open wheel racing back to the forefront.

Last week, I featured some of the photographs I had taken during the Thunder telecast series. I will have some more to share with you this week. Stop by and take a look, as they will bring back some memories, from this great era we enjoyed at our track. The Thunder series was also what got me started in doing the Thunderhead line of racing apparel. Dave Despain, would open the show with, "Welcome, all of you Thunderheads out there." Hence, the Thunderhead name, and all that followed, has certainly been an interesting trip.

MAY DAY

"The Month of May"—I remember when it was the biggest month of the year, culminating in the running of the "Big One" at the Indianapolis Motor Speedway on Memorial Day. I couldn't wait to hear it on the radio with Sid Collins calling all the action in such a way that one could picture in their mind the actual event as it unfolded.

Then a miracle of modern science was introduced, with closed circuit broadcasting of the race. My father and I went down to see the race live at the Olympic Auditorium in living black and white. There was a giant screen for all to see…what a sight!

So much has changed over the years. Now you can watch it on your own big screen TV in the comfort of your home in full color and surround sound. Those great radio commentators with their descriptive insights are gone, but not forgotten, by us old timers.

The cars have also changed, with cookie-cutter road rockets taking the place of individual designs, by true car designers. This has, over the years, made the whole deal a little on the boring side. Fortunately, they seem to have recognized this, and will be making changes in the near future. New management has taken over and has a "bull riding" mentality that just might work in bringing back the luster of the Indy Car Series. I certainly hope so. Bringing back the good old days is always a topic of discussion between old timers, however, times change, and these will someday be the "good old days" to our younger set.

"WHAT IS, IS"

Tough times are upon us in many ways. Just look around and you will see all of the signs of very tough economic situations facing everyone in one way or another. Empty commercial buildings and foreclosed homes are just a few of the signs that times are tough. The future does not hold much promise, as prospects for a recovery seem distant at best.

This brings up thoughts about our racetrack and what it provides. It is comprised of both fans and racers who come together each week to enjoy one of the most exciting sports ever. *The Star* featured an article recently, about the tough times the drivers and teams were having in keeping up with expenses. This is a matter of fact that cannot be denied, as racing is a very expensive endeavor. In addition, the fans are not showing up, which results in smaller gate money, which results in lower purses. "What is, is." As fans, we share some responsibility in the success or failure of our much needed racing fix each week. Let us all consider how we, as fans, can help out in bolstering the attendance. Bringing your friends or neighbors to an event would be a good start. We need to take some responsibility in keeping our sport alive, and not treat it like our personal secret pastime. Next week, bringing a friend should be your goal. Support this place, as it supports you and your passion for the sport.

As I travel this week to Speed Week in Oregon and Washington, I find every track is facing the same dilemma. We, as fans, need to take charge of our future or it may be gone. Face it, "What is, is. There is no denying it.

FAIR BREAK

Every year we take a break for the Ventura County Fair. It seems to be a perfect time for all of the racers to regroup and get set for the final run to the finish. Who knows what will take place when racing resumes at the end of August? Only time will tell if the leaders will hold on, or will someone charge up to be a spoiler for the championships.

Racing in California is mainly held on fairground tracks. This is also true in other states and the history of racing is founded at the local fairgrounds. Population growth has been the culprit over these many years causing the closing of many tracks. Somehow, the fairground facilities have managed to survive. Looking back, we had Oxnard Speedway, Carpenteria Thunderbowl, Saugus Speedway, Gardena, Culver City, and many other tracks too numerous to count. Today, in California, racing is mainly held at fairground tracks. Chico, Petaluma, Antioch, Placerville, Ventura, Perris, Chowchilla, and others have somehow survived in the modern world. We, as fans should be grateful that the racing tradition has survived in our area. I will be heading out to Knoxville, Iowa for the Nationals in August. If you live in Knoxville, you have to be a race fan or else. This is a town of 7,000 people with the fairgrounds right in the middle of the city. It holds a stadium that seats 25,000 people and the National Sprint Car Hall of Fame. It has become the mecca of Sprint Car racing and deservedly so. The town lives for the Nationals and each year fans return from all over the world for a gathering that is really something to see. It is a shame that the city of Ventura does not have this same love of our sport as they do. Ventura is truly missing out on a treasure sitting in their own backyard. Have fun at the Fair and we will see all of you when racing resumes on August 27th.

ON THE ROAD AGAIN

I am "BACK ON THE ROAD AGAIN," which is also the song I play by Willie Nelson, whenever I hit the road for another adventure. This time, I am off to Calistoga and Chico for some big events on the racing calendar. Calistoga is great and all of the stuff surrounding it makes it special. First is the surrounding towns of Napa Valley, which is one beautiful place. Just the drive up from Highway 80 is beautiful. It takes you back in time with the quaint shops and wineries lining the road. Life seems slower in this valley, at least from an outsiders view.

The racing was great and former "Rising Star" winner Jonathan Henry won the Midget main on Sunday night. He seems to have found a home in that red Midget and the results on the big half-mile were impressive. Mike Spencer won the Sprint Car feature, so it was a good night for the SO CAL guys. You should try and make this trip next year, as it is really a fun weekend for any race fan.

As write this, I am now in Chico for the 50th Annual Gold Cup Race of Champions. This year, the event features a full array of non-wing Sprint Cars along with Midgets and the World of Outlaws. A four night deal, that really brings out a big crowd, and a lot of atmosphere to the event. I will have photos next week when I return to Ventura.

Meanwhile, we have our golf outing next Friday, the 16th and we would sure like to have you be a player either in real golf or Golf N' Stuff. Either event you choose will be a blast and the dinner and party to follow is always a winner. Email me a let me know if you can make it as it will be a good time for all . . . See you there . . . Tom

200,000 MILES

As I breezed into Chico for the Gold Cup, the odometer on the Thunder Van passed the 200,000 mile mark. I think that a car should last at least 300,000 miles, if it is cared for with good service. In a way, the life of your car and your own life seem to be on a parallel trip.

Think about it. Life can be broken down into thirds, and so can the life of your car. The first third of life (or 100,000 miles) is the creative part. Your life dreams and passions are created between the ages of seven and ten years old. This is also the dream and passionate stage of car ownership.

The second third of life is usually spent either chasing the dream/passion, or getting sidetracked or misdirected, away from our true life mission. This can lead to a life of quiet desperation, and if not caught early, can be a heavy load, and result in both physical and mental problems. The same holds true if you stray away from taking care of your car. Lack of service can lead to hidden problems down the road.

The final third of life is the most mysterious. We do not know how long it will be, just as we don't know if the car will reach the desired 300,000 miles. Did we follow our dreams or did we get sidetracked along the way? Is it too late to find our true passion? I, for one, say it is never too late to reach for the stars. The miles go by at a rapid rate, so don't wait.

THE END IS NEAR

It seems as though the season just started, and when I look at the calendar, it is almost over. This year started out with much fear and trepidation about the economy, and how it would affect the racing, at various venues in our region. I consider our region to be the West Coast and that includes Oregon and Washington along with Arizona and Nevada.

After having visited tracks in all of those states, I have come to the following conclusion. Race fans and drivers seem to have very much in common throughout our region, when it comes to attitudes and beliefs. To a person, they all know how to run a program or series, better than the promoter at their individual track. This should not be surprising! We tend to become experts at whatever it is we like. Even though, we probably have no clue as to what it takes to run an event, a race team, or whatever the endeavor happens to be. Drivers complain about the purses being too small for their investment. Fans complain about ticket prices and the cost of gas to get to the races. In reality, the purses have not risen, nor have the ticket prices paid by the fans. Something is terribly wrong with a sport, that has the fans paying almost nothing to attend. You can't compare it to football, basketball, NASCAR, etc. We are, in reality, a club sport that is a lot like Polo. Very expensive toys ridden and watched, by a select group of people, who happen to enjoy the process.

Tough economic times add stress to everyone's life. The promoter's, the race teams, and the fans should recognize this. Things are not going to get better economically in the near future. It is time for all of us to work together in order to keep our sport alive until better times return.

PRINT MEDIA

The Times They Are A-Changin' is an old song that is even more relevant today than ever before. Last week, I opened my recent issue of *National Speed Sport News* and a very disturbing message was written on page four of this issue. This would be the last issue to be published of this stalwart publication. For nearly 70 years, *National Speed Sport News* has brought the latest auto racing news and opinions to mailboxes across this nation and the world. I, for one, always looked forward to the excellent articles and opinion columns that graced this publication. No other form of media covered our sport quite like they did.

Yes, the world is changing! For us old folks, it is not a change for the better, just change that will affect our way of life. Today, information is available instantly on the Internet. The younger people have gravitated to having the world in the palm of their hand. Still, there was something special about holding and folding a newspaper while enjoying a cup of coffee on the patio. I guess I will have to get an iPod or a Kindle, in order to keep up with what is going on in the world. Next in line to disappear will be the *L.A. Times* and most other newspapers that are struggling to stay alive in this modern age. They can call it progress, but I wonder, is it really?

Ventura Raceway Articles

2012

PATRON OF THE ARTS

Across the world and in the United States, Patrons of the Arts fund museums, artists, musicians and other artistic endeavors. If you visit the Carnegie Museum in Oxnard, you will find ongoing efforts to promote art and artists. The museum was funded by the Carnegie trust, which funds museums across the whole country. The Getty trust built a mammoth structure in Los Angeles, which houses one of the world's largest collections of art and photography. These are just two of many foundations that do similar funding for the artistic world in various artistic fields. If you go way back in time, Mozart, Van Gough and others were funded by churches and other patrons of the arts. Without this funding, the art world would not exist in today's world.

The Sprint Car and other forms of open wheel racing face a dilemma. If you consider the world of racing an art form, which I do, then where does it stand in today's economic climate? Small tracks and drivers across the country are faced with rising costs which have led to reduced fields and facilities. Let's face it, the cost of funding a race team or running a race track far outweighs the return on the investment needed to survive in today's world.

Where are the Patrons of the Arts, which the race world needs in this time of economic stress? Some do exist, such as Tony Stewart and Kasey Kane, who fund teams in several of the racing series across the country. The race community needs a Getty or Carnegie if it is to prosper and grow in the coming years. If none step up, then we will be faced with the reality of smaller fields and fewer tracks in which to enjoy our art form. Yes, the racing will still be good. However, we will all lose in the long run as some great artist's (drivers) will never get to share their art with the world.

LEAVING AMARILLO

Leaving Amarillo, on my return trip from the Chili Bowl is always an interesting and thought provoking part of the journey. Amarillo is in the Texas Panhandle, which is probably one of the most desolate parts of the country. The wind always blows and the temperature is always down in the 40s. The panhandle is all cattle country and there must be at least thirty steak house restaurants on the main road. Not one of which I have found to be very good. There is not a tree in sight, which leaves a horizon as far as the eye can see. The Cadillac Ranch, a unique art piece, is on the left and the old Route 66 runs on the right. On Route 66 you can see the skeletons of days gone by. Broken dreams left rotting in the sun with no one to tell their stories. I wonder what became of all those dreams that people had on their journey through this life. Did they just move on to other dreams, or were their lives shattered, and left to die along this long and desolate highway? We will never know of course, as no one is left to tell the tale.

Dirt tracks, of which we are very fond, have also traveled this route. Across our nation lie the skeletons of days gone by. Dirt tracks proliferated everywhere, in both large and small towns, with fans gathering on the weekend, to share in their love of dirt track racing. Only a few have survived to still run today, and they all face a battle of survival in a world that is changing at a very fast pace. We, as fans, need to take action in order to keep our sport alive for future generations. Our sport is followed by a demographic of older people. The time is now, for all of us to bring younger fans into the fold. Yes, it is up to us to ensure the future, or we will join the skeletons along Route 66, just broken dreams rotting in the sun.

ON THE ROAD AGAIN

Track thirteen on my Willie Nelson CD is "On The Road Again." This classic Willie tune is the one I start each trip on as it is appropriate for the travels ahead. I followed the World of Outlaws on their western swing and the song fits the journey. Las Vegas, Perris, Tulare, Merced, Chico, Calistoga were supposed to be the stops along the trail. However, Mother Nature played a big part in the lack of racing for all concerned. Rain cancelled out Tulare, Chico, and Calistoga. This made for a very costly trip for me and the traveling Outlaws along with the promoters who staged the events. All of us returned home disappointed with not having what should have been a banner month.

I am back home and looking forward to tonight's show which features the Mighty Midgets along with the other divisions. The economy is one subject that I found everyone talking about on my trip. The cost of racing is going up and each racer faces this hard fact every week they try and pay the bills and compete at our track. I am starting a new project which should be fun and help raise money for one unlucky racer each week. Stop by and play the "Thunderhead Bean Bag Toss Game." Make a donation of $5 and the winner will receive a free Thunderhead T-Shirt for their effort. All of the money will be donated to a Hard Luck Driver of the night with all divisions being eligible. This should be a fun event and help out a driver who needs some dough to repair the damage and be able to run next time. Your participation is needed in these tough times we are facing.

THIS N' THAT

Our new weekly "Bean Bag for Bucks" raised $135 last week and that money will be used to help some unlucky driver repair his or her race car . . . It was fun, so stop by and play the "Bean Bag" game again this week . . . I am now on Facebook and these articles will be posted soon on a weekly basis . . . Loved having the band play last week. It brought a party atmosphere to the track. I hope we get more of this as the season progresses. If you know of a band that would like to get some publicity, let me know . . . I noticed on Facebook that David Thunderhead, yes, look him up, changed his last name to Thunderhead. Now, that is brand imaging at its best . . . I am looking forward to my next journey which will run from Chico to Skagit with a week of Sprint Car racing in three states the first week of June . . . Tulare will have a two-day show on May 11/12, featuring wing and non-wing cars . . . Thunderhead will be there. It is the Chris and Brian Faria Memorial weekend and always draws a big crowd of fans and cars . . . Most fun is watching the "Vintage Super Mods" on Saturday night. They are worth the trip by themselves. How do you like the new track configuration here at Ventura? . . . I think it is a good move and the racing should get even better as the drivers figure it out. I received my first issue of the new *National Speed Sport News* and am pleased to say that it is a winner. All of us cried when the original weekly paper died last March. Please subscribe to this new monthly version so it will stay alive for us paper lovers. Last, but not least, I have two seats available for the Chili Bowl! Let me know if you are interested . . . Primo seat location in the main grandstand for all nights . . . Enjoy the show.

CHANGE

What used to be the Month of May is now the two weeks of May. The Indianapolis 500 was once the biggest event in motorsports, however, it is now just a blip on the racing calendar. What once was an eagerly anticipated event has dwindled down to an international day of mourning for most of us who remember the significance of this event.

Gone are the American heroes that filled the field and raced to the cheers of their respective fans. Mario Andretti, Parnelli Jones, A.J. Foyt, Johnny Rutherford, Al Unser, Al Unser Jr., Rick Mears, Bobby Unser and other great names from the past are just a distant memory of what was once the greatest spectacle in racing. To a man, they were also local heroes from the short track racing world that covered this country from coast to coast. Today, we have an international field of drivers to which most American race fans have little knowledge. The Indy series has turned into an American mini version of Formula One, with mostly road races on city streets as their featured events. No longer will some local favorite get a chance to make it to the "Big Show" that would endear them to racing fans across the country.

They say that change is good. In this case, change has left a great event a shadow of its former self. A lot of things are changing in this world, however, some things are best left unchanged.

A "NATURAL"

Looking back in time, we all have watched the latest and greatest athletes go from a small venue, to being on top of the world in their respective sports. I remember a few from our area such as Corey Pavin who became one of the PGA's top golfers. Then there was Ken McMullen, drafted by the Dodgers and going on to a stellar major league baseball career. They, along with many others were called "naturals" because they made it seem so easy to excel in their given sport. It seems as though they were born with abilities that far exceed the norm and takes them to a level few can achieve.

Last weekend, at the Tulare Thunderbowl, the latest "natural" showed up and almost swept both divisions of the two-day event. Kyle Larson, all of nineteen years of age, has shown all of the big dogs how to run a Sprint Car. He ran both the King of the West 410 Winged Sprinters and the Non-Wing 360 Divisions. Sweeping both races on Friday night, he returned in a borrowed 360, starting 20th in the main, and passed them all for a thrilling win over Bud Kaeding and other top stars. Leading the winged main, his motor blew with four laps to go or he would have had a clean sweep. This kid is really something special, and I am sure we will be seeing him on TV someday soon running with NASCAR. When he arrives, he will be following in the footsteps of others that have gone before him. Tony Stewart and Jeff Gordon, were two of the best "naturals" of all time. Now, they will have to look over their shoulders for the next one.

RITE OF PASSAGE

Looking back in time, there is one thing that is sorely missing in most of our communities. That, my friends, is the barber shop. The barber shop was a central meeting place for the men of the town. It was where you heard all about what was going on in your town. It was where you heard all of the gossip. It was where you would grow up and eventually become one of the adults who took part in the discussions. As a kid, you were just a listener, but listening gave you a sense of being part of something.

Today, for the most part, the meeting place has been replaced by a salon, or salon attitude. You make an appointment, arrive, get a haircut and leave, without seeing another person. This, to me, is a sad state of affairs. Young people today do not get that "right of passage" that unbeknownst to them is a real life lesson of untold value. I guess you could say that they will post getting a haircut on their Facebook. Somehow, that does not seem to cut it in the life experience department, but maybe I just don't get it.

The racing world is unique, in that it still has a rite of passage that is alive and working in today's world. Whether a racer or a fan, kids today still get that great life lesson with their peers, parents or grandparents. We have seen it here at the raceway many times. From Jr. Dwarf to Full Modified, from Jr. Midget to Pro Sprint Car, from fan to pit crew member, the passage goes on. So, enjoy whatever part of the passage you are involved with. Someday, it will all take place on your phone.

OLD SCHOOL

If you missed last weeks Midget main event, then you missed one of the best demonstrations of driving a Midget Car I have seen in a very long time. Wally Pankratz, a 67-year-old veteran put on a show that will go down in memory as a true clinic in driving expertise. Lap after lap, Wally displayed skill's that only come with years of experience, and an innate ability to read a track and other driver's moves. Not only did he dominate, he did so with clean moves that every young driver should try and emulate. This demonstrated the way a racer should run an event. Only a blown radiator stopped him from winning the race, which was a barn burner of the highest caliber.

We hear a lot of talk about the old days, both in racing and other aspects of life. Route 66 has a historic charisma about life in a slower lane. Old Las Vegas had its lounge shows that people still remember as the best of times for that city and its visitors. Both are examples of a time gone by that may never be again. Racing was also different then, as drivers did not have the safety features of today, which in some cases leads to more dangerous moves to make a pass. Wally, once again, showed us that you don't have to crash out your rivals to get by them. Smart, cunning moves made this show a great one. Thank you, Wally, for showing us that old school is still alive and well in this modern world.

SPEED WEEK

I am missing in action this week as I am working the Winged Sprint Cars Tour to the Dirt Cup in Skagit. The tour began at Chico on Friday night with racing in Medford, Oregon on Saturday night. Both Chico, and Medford had good car counts and exciting racing. Tim Kaeding and Jonathan Allard split the wins as they usually do. Sunday night in Cottage Grove, Oregon, it was all Tim Kaeding on the little Bull Ring. (Do you suspect a pattern here?) The tour moves on to Willamette Speedway in Lebanon, Oregon on Sunday night and then Gray's Harbor in Elma, Washington on Tuesday night. It wraps up with three days of the Dirt Cup at Skagit Speedway up in Burlington, Washington. Total round trip, 1,600 miles, eight nights of Sprint Car action, and seeing a lot of old friends along the way. (Might make a good song lyric.)

About that pattern mentioned above. Sprint Car racing, like life itself, is made up of various factions, usually set apart by financial standings. Tim and Jonathan, both very exciting drivers, are sponsored by big money people, who spare no expense in winning equipment. That, as in life, leaves the rest of the pack struggling to catch a break. Fair or not, that is what life is all about, so accept it as fact. The problem these days, is that the lower rungs (less funding), team counts are dwindling. Unable to travel, the car counts will dwindle as the tour progresses. This leaves behind the rest of the field, which is needed to make it a good show. This, will also affect the whole season, which leaves our sport in a precarious position. Will the sport be able to survive the economic mess we find ourselves in, or will it just fade into our memory banks as the "good old days?"

SPEED WEEK (PART TWO)

Leaving Chico and heading north one comes across the 14,000 foot high, snow capped behemoth, known as Mount Shasta. It is always something to behold, and is just the beginning of a beautiful run through southern Oregon. Trees and rivers line the highway as far as the eye can see, making for scenic beauty that is unsurpassed. Medford and the Southern Oregon Speedway were the first stop on Saturday night with Cottage Grove on Sunday. I did not work the Cottage Grove event and chose to play golf and hang with my friends for the day and evening. The golf course runs along a river and the pits of the race track, and is a very peaceful place to spend the day. The track itself is a very old facility that will soon be razed and replaced with a modern facility. The racing was good as it is a Bull Ring and always delivers.

Willamette was next on the agenda and it has just been completely renovated by Jerry Schram. It is by far the best appearing facility I have seen in Sprint Car racing, and should set the bar very high for others to follow. The next night at Gray's Harbor, Washington was rained out, so I headed north to Skagit for the Dirt Cup, which is the major event of the tour. I checked in at the Whispering Firs Motel in Alger, which is three miles from the track, ready for three nights of Sprint Car racing. Sitting in the gazebo having coffee and planning the three days ahead, I was able to see a Bald Eagle fly by, and what a site it was. The race track itself sits in a forest and the views from the grandstand are spectacular. I have posted a photo on my Facebook, so take a look. Even though the Saturday night finale rained out, it was still a good week and the fan count was high along with the 38 Sprint Cars to put on a great show.

Speed Week covers three states and six race tracks, drawing good car counts and a very large fan base. It is a shame that we can't have something like it in Southern California. We tend to blame it on the traffic congestion, but that is just an excuse, as the hard core fans in other areas make it a vacation week, each and every year.

LIKE A BAND OF GYPSIES

Like a band of Gypsies, Willie Nelson and Family rolled into Agoura Hills for a gig at the Canyon Club. Their tour bus, Honeysuckle Rose, carries the legendary Willie and his eclectic troop on an endless tour of the nation. Stopping to entertain the folks at both large and small venues, all of which sell out to capacity, he never fails to deliver a sterling performance. His performances go nonstop for an hour and a half. Filled with songs of varying styles, from country to jazz, that he plays on his old guitar named Trigger, the show is filled with diversity that is unmatched in the music world. He is backed up by a group of musicians that is second to none, many of whom have been with him for decades. By backing up, I mean that is what they do, not, overwhelming the audience with drums and guitars blasting out the vocals, as many younger bands do today. At 75 years old, we may not be able to enjoy this national icon for too many more years. Time catches up to all of us and someday this treasure will be gone. Try and catch him next time and see what a true life passion is all about.

The Sprint Car world has a similar scenario what with Steve Kinser and Sammy Swindell rolling down the highway year after year, on their endless pursuit of racing excellence. Stopping at large and small venues, there are crowds that come out to see their giant race rigs roll into town, knowing that the night will bring out the best in both. Anticipation builds throughout the day and these fans are never disappointed with the show they see that night. They are just a couple of legends enjoying the pursuit of their life passion, and sharing it with the world.

Willie, Steve, and Sammy have given it their all. Which brings up the question: Have we given it our all? Something to think about.

GREAT SPECTACLE

Each year in August, the Sprint Car world gathers in Knoxville, Iowa, for the Knoxville Nationals. This yearly event has been going on for 52 years and gets better each year. If you are a fan of Sprint Car racing, it is a must-visit for your bucket list. Both wing and non-wing cars compete over a ten-day period which features the elite of the Sprint Car teams from the United States, New Zealand, Canada, and Australia. The feature event on Saturday night is one great spectacle. The opening ceremonies feature a Knoxville local with a beautiful voice singing the New Zealand, Australian, and United States anthems. This, along with the fireworks and the four-abreast salute to the crowd is something every fan should experience at least once. After the opening ceremonies, 24 Sprint Cars compete for 50 laps in a mad dash for the biggest prize in Sprint Car racing. The winner is enshrined in a special group that includes some of the all-time greats of our sport.

One of the highlights of the trip is a visit to the National Sprint Car Hall of Fame. This group, headed by Bob Baker and Tom Schmeh have put together a spectacular display, featuring the legends of our sport, and documented history of all things related to Sprint Car racing. Each year that I attend this event, the Hall of Fame is the highlight of the trip. At the very least, you should become a supporting member of this great organization. Stop by the Thunderhead booth tonight and pick up an application for membership. They need all of our support. Better yet, plan a trip next year to the Nationals. You won't regret it. By the way, California has more inductees enshrined in the Hall of Fame than any other state.

BACK HOME AGAIN

I just returned from a ten-day swing through northern California following the USAC 410 series and World of Outlaws. It all started with the Louie Vermeil Classic in Calistoga on Labor Day weekend. This is always a great event and this years held up their reputation. Tom and Jeanie Hunt promote this event each year, and each year it gets better. Calistoga is a great place to visit, what with the Hot Springs and a picturesque town, filled with great shops and restaurants. My favorite on Friday night is Brannan's Grill, which features great Jazz and food to match. The race track is a big, classic half-mile which always brings about some awesome racing, and this year was no exception. I highly recommend that you put this event on your bucket list for next year. You will not be disappointed.

Chico's Silver Dollar Speedway was next with the 59th running of the Gold Cup. Sprint Car fans arrived from all over, including Hawaii, Canada, and too many states to mention here. When I say Sprint Car fans, I mean these people are not just fans, they are fanatics. Most of them have been attending this event for many years. The camp grounds were full of everything from tents to motor homes and a party atmosphere prevailed for all four days. The BBQ's were in full swing each day, a golf tournament was held on Friday, and they still prevail in the politically incorrect world, with a bikini contest on Friday night. It is just one big party for four days with great racing each night. The World of Outlaws are a big part of the show, and a local hero was able to once again take the big money on Saturday night. Kyle Larson nearly lapped the field and further enhanced his image as the next big racing star to come out of the Sprint Car world.

It is good to be back. I am looking forward to our big event on September 29, when we will be hosting Zoey's Café and the Dr. Surf band for our Battle at the Beach Midget Classic. Plan on it, so maybe we can show the northern California folks that we know how to party!

SURF'S UP

I missed being here last week, due to the fact that I was working at the beach during the Surf Contest. I attended this function with the intention of bringing together two niche sports. As most of you know, just 100 yards from the raceway, is some of the best surfing areas in the world. One of our drivers, Bruce Douglas, is also quite well-known in the surfing community and competes in all of the local contests. In addition to being located side by side at this beautiful beach location, these two sports, surfing and racing, share a very common lifestyle. Both the competitors and fans of each sport are quite unique. They live and breathe their respective sports and most have been doing it for a lifetime. The competitors on both sides hate to lose and give it their all when competing for a win. I met many of their community and invited them to our upcoming Battle at the Beach Midget Classic which will run on Saturday, September 29. This event has been expanded to include Zoey's Café, who, along with our Thunderhead brand is sponsoring the Dr. Surf band. Dr. Surf will perform at the raceway on Saturday night and also in a very special get together at noon Sunday at Zoey's Café. This will be a great opportunity for all of you fans and racers to meet and have some fun. You might just meet a few surfers, which could be interesting to say the least. So, mark your calendars and help make this a memorable event that could become a yearly tradition.

THE PAST

National Speed Sport News in its day was the Bible of motorsports. Myself, and a legion of racing fans looked forward to getting it each week. Inside was everything you needed to know about the goings on in motorsports at every level. The most interesting column was always *Editors Notebook* written by Chris Economaki. Each week he would bring you up-to-date with details of so many varied happenings, that it boggled your mind that one person could be so attuned to the happenings around the world. The editor, Chris Economaki, passed away recently at the age of 91, leaving behind a legacy that will never be equaled.

Chris Economaki began his career peddling single copies of the paper at age 13 and eventually became the editor of the publication for 60 years. His history is filled with both print, radio, and television, and he knew racing and knew how to speak about it. He will be missed as we make the transformation into the digital age, leaving behind his world of print on paper.

Young people today, in this troubled economic world would behoove themselves to take a lesson from this old master. Note that he started at the bottom in a field he loved, willing to do anything in order to be a part of it. When you follow your life passion, it is not work, it is like being on vacation every day. Rest in Peace Chris, you will be missed.

ARE YOU A MEMBER?

You proudly call yourselves Sprint Car fans and tell everyone that it is the greatest sport ever. You attend as many Sprint Car races as possible and wish you could attend them all. You dream of going to Indiana Sprint Week, love the Oval Nationals and follow the sport on every web site you can find. You follow your favorites on Facebook and probably have a Facebook page of your own where you espouse your love of the sport for all to see. Another dream week on your bucket list is probably the Knoxville Nationals, which you say you must go to someday. The list of 'I want to go to...' is very long and few of us, if any, will fulfill the dream.

Another spot on the list is seeing the National Sprint Car Hall of Fame, and taking in all of the history they have archived for your pleasure. It is just amazing to wander the aisles and get lost in the history of the sport we proudly call our own. The motto of the Hall of Fame is "Promoting the Future, by Preserving the Past." So I ask you, are you a member of the National Sprint Car Hall of Fame? Do you truly call yourself a Sprint Car fan? Do you really care about the "future" or the "history" of your sport? You can become a member for as little as $25 per year by going to www.sprintcarhof.com or call (800) 874-4488. Once you join you will be a member in good standing, supporting the sport you say you love. Of course, you could leave joining on your "bucket list" of things to do for another year or so. This gets you membership in the "Hall of Shame" along with all of the "someday I am going to do that" crowd. So join now, you won't regret it.

Ventura Raceway Articles

2013

Dr. Thunderhead

MIDGET MANIA

It has been many years since I saw my first Midget race. From the beginning, it became my favorite form of racing, even ahead of the Sprint Cars. There is just something about Midgets on a small bull ring that stirs excitement and gets my pulse rate up. I have discussed this with drivers, and they agree. There is nothing like a Midget car they can man-handle around and its response is quick and just a lot of fun to drive.

Thinking back to the glory days of Thursday Night Thunder, there wasn't a more exciting series than those battles at the beach. Ventura was the center of that great series and tonight we have a chance to relive some of the Midget action we so coveted back in the day. Every Midget show this year has been a barn burner and tonight's race should be no exception. On my recent trip to the Gold Cup, they had a Midget night and they put on a show that was amazing. All of the top drivers at that event will be here tonight. So hold on to your seat, it should be a good one.

As for the future of Midget racing, it is in a very precarious position. Costs have skyrocketed and car counts are low, which endangers the future of this great sport. Of course, the Chili Bowl continues to draw every Midget Car in the world. However, that is only once a year, and that is not healthy for the sport. Long term, we need some changes in order to draw more teams into the fold. Maybe a return to the VW-based motor would bring down the cost of racing. Sadly, it might do so in the beginning. However, based on past experience, the teams would figure out a way to make them expensive. I guess it is just human nature.

SAFETY

A tragic accident occurred recently at Marysville Raceway which involved an out of control Sprint Car careening off the track exit. Two people were killed in this situation when they were not watching the track. Racing is a dangerous sport for anyone in attendance and especially for those who work in the various positions of helping create the program. We all need to be aware of the dangers that are around us and act accordingly to ensure our safety. As fans, we are invited to visit the pit area after the races and visit with our favorite drivers and crew members. Let's not take this privilege lightly. Be aware that equipment is being loaded and cars moved around and it is up to us to watch out for our own safety. If you take children along with you it is even more imperative that you watch out for their safety.

The Ventura Raceway Safety Crew is one of the best I have seen at any track I have visited. They are a super group, that are very skilled at what they do. Their response time and skill at handling their duties rank with the very best. Let's give them a "HIGH FIVE" the next time you see them. They do a superb job and deserve praise.

Have a safe evening and enjoy the great racing that takes place here at Ventura Raceway.

THE ROAR OF ENGINES

Looking back in time, it was the roar of engines that grabbed my attention at an early age. Growing up with hot rods and glass pack mufflers is engrained in my memory and probably contributed to the lack of hearing quality that I have today. The roar of Sprint Cars and the scream of Midgets were what attracted me and others to the sport of auto racing. It was just part of the deal, and the rumble of my V-8 Mustang still brings back memories of the past.

Times, They Are A Changin', is a famous old statement. It is even more relevant today than ever before. They have just announced the forming of Formula E races. Open wheel electric race cars are scheduled to race in Los Angeles, along with nine other cities around the world, in 2014. Just imagine, no sound except that of screeching tires. Somehow, it just doesn't seem like racing, without the roar of engines to accent the action. However, I will try and keep an open mind about this change in the world order of things. Other things have changed and we have survived, and in some ways are better off with the changes. Cell phones, computers, email, and other stuff are now what future generations will be remembering down the road. Somehow, I still think the sounds and smells of the internal combustion engine are not replaceable by silence. Time will tell.

THE BIG LEAGUES

"What went wrong?" you ask. Why hasn't Sprint Car/Midget racing become the premier type of racing events in the country? They are, without a doubt, the most exciting form of racing today, and have been, since they began many years ago. It is mind boggling to see what other forms of racing have risen to in terms of dollars and prestige.

USAC ruled the racing world back in the day: The INDY 500, Champ Cars, Sprint Cars, Midgets, and Stock Cars. However, their luster has gone by the wayside. NASCAR took over and drove it into one of the top sporting events in the country. Try as they might, it never clicked for USAC. They remain a grass-roots organization, with many various regional series splintered around the country. Just imagine, what a dynamic marketing program might have brought to this great sport. Today, they need to add the word "extreme" to their marketing campaign. After all, Sprint Cars and Midgets were the original extreme form of sports. The youth of today would flock to see them, and this is what is needed for the sport to continue. I attended the rebirth of Sprint Car racing at Orange Show last week and saw a big crowd of mostly gray beards. Our sport needs a youth movement in order to continue on and grow in the status it deserves. Who will be the one who makes it happen?

WHAT IF?

I took the grand kids to Circus Vargas last week for our annual trip to the Big Top. As usual, they put on a great show. The circus has evolved over time into a unique entertainment experience for audiences of all ages. In the past, there were many of these traveling extravaganzas. Over time they have evolved into just a few left to practice their art. Ringling Brothers, Barnum & Bailey is an example of several shows combining into one major operation. Economics played a key role in the evolution of the circus as we know it today.

Imagine if the Sprint Car and Midget racing world could evolve into something that would be similar in nature to the circus. In California, we could have the CRA. The California Racing Association would govern the schedule and promote the circuit at venues throughout the state. As it stands today, you have individual promoters, along with several associations, fighting for a dwindling car count. No one wins in this situation. Not the promoters, not the drivers and certainly not the fans. A true ruling body would mean larger car counts, larger fan attendance, and in the long run, more money for all concerned. There is not enough room in this column to go into detail, however, the idea is worth talking about. The circus survived and thrives today, because they adapted to a changing economic world. What if our world did the same? One can just imagine . . .

THE MIDGETS

Tonight, we get a real treat with the combined forces of the USAC and the VRA Midgets. As I wrote last week, the need for a California series is quite evident in this sport. There are not enough cars in the state to have three series' (when you count in the BCRA) and racing suffers from this demise. Economics played a major role in bringing this situation to be what it is today. A while back, Midgets were powered by VW motors, which were affordable to a large number of racers who could afford to go racing and be competitive in the sport. Then, a couple of guys with deep pockets spent a small fortune building more powerful motors. This created a racing class of have's and have not's. Those without deep pockets slowly dropped out of the sport and we are now left with around 25 cars in the whole state. In addition, they created the pavement car style that chased away another group of car owners and drivers. Somehow, Midget racing has survived, even though it is only a shadow of its former glory days.

Willie Nelson turned 80 this year and still tours the country entertaining his legions of fans. With the use of a 60-year-old guitar, he has become a national icon. His guitar has the nickname of Trigger and will someday be enshrined in the Smithsonian as a national treasure. Midget racing had the same potential. However, in its constant search for the next great trick motor, it will someday die off into oblivion. Sad to say, but the truth is in the pudding.

THE BLOOM IS OFF THE ROSE

Many years ago, Memorial Day was the biggest day for motorsports. The Indy 500 was the premier racing event in the world. Fans worldwide would wait with anticipation for this great spectacle of speed. The *L.A. Times* had Jim Murray on site for the entire month of May. His daily reports were full of clever quips that made him a legend as a sports reporter.

This year, I am sad to report that the *L.A. Times* had almost no pre-race coverage, other than a few notes, in the etc. section on the back page. What was once an all-American event is now just another race. Many years ago, the road to Indy was via Midgets, Sprint Cars, and Champ Cars. This is no longer the case, as only big money sponsorship gets a driver into the race in today's world. The days of great American heroes, the likes of Parnelli Jones, A.J. Foyt, Tony Bettenhausen, Bill Vukovich, the Unsers and many others are but a distant memory. The road to Indy has closed and will never return. Bump Day was attended by fewer fans than we had here at Ventura last weekend. The race itself was excellent, with little or no carnage to spoil the event. However, a "yellow flag" finish is something that leaves a lot to be desired for the race fans. A green-white-checker would have made it a spectacular event. The bloom is off the rose, for what was once, a great American event.

NO ROOM AT THE TOP (PART ONE)

I went to the Johnny Cash Revival last weekend at the Fairgrounds. This event has become quite a spectacle, with many groups honoring the legendary entertainer. My main purpose was to see Jr. Brown. Jr. Brown is a renowned guitar player and singer/song writer/artist with a dry wit sense of humor. He is an amazing talent and like others at this level of the industry has a cult following. One wonders why, with all of his talent, he is not a national sensation. He is probably best known for his song "Highway Patrol," which every Highway Patrol officer I have met has heard, and they love it. In addition, he and Jimmy Hendrix are probably the two best guitar players you will ever hear.

So, why is Hendrix known worldwide and Jr. Brown only has a cult following. Hendrix died years ago at an early age and Jr. Brown is now over sixty, still trudging along on the second tier of the music world. Somehow, this does not make sense, but it is reality. In the real world, there is only room at the top for a select number of talents. Sorry, but that is the fact that all of the people who seek stardom must face.

Take NASCAR as an example. There is room for only 43 drivers in the top division and everyone else, no matter how talented, must fight over the crumbs left over in the lower divisions. The same rule applies to football, basketball, baseball, soccer, hockey, golf, music, movies. The list goes on and on. Reaching the top wrung in any of these endeavors, takes more than just talent.

NO ROOM AT THE TOP (PART TWO)

The open wheel world of Sprint Car and Midget racing is no different than any other form of entertainment. Across this country are some of the most talented race drivers, grinding away each week, seeking stardom in the big leagues of motor racing. Only a select few will reach the elusive brass ring and the pot of gold it releases. Over the years, we have seen the likes of Page Jones, in my opinion, one of the most talented drivers of his era. His career ended, with a brutal crash, just as he was about to grab the ring.

Recently, we lost one of the best ever. Jason Lefler came closer than most to making it to the big time. His career started here at Ventura Raceway in a Midget, and he built a cult following of fans who appreciated his talent. Like Jr. Brown, one step away from that elusive brass ring. When the announcer called his name, the fans knew they were in for a spectacular show and he always delivered. We will miss him and others lost to the dangers of this spectacular sport.

Truth be known, we probably prefer our heroes to stay in the lower level. Small venues, up close and personal, seem to be better than the big arenas, where you have to look from afar. Jr. Brown in the Staples Arena would lose some of that aura and mystique that we enjoy so much. When Tim Keading leaves to travel with the Outlaws, a void is left in Northern California Sprint Car racing. I doubt that Kyle Larson will be allowed to continue at the local dirt track any longer, as he is just about to grab the brass ring. The rising stars on the second level may be the best show you will see, no matter what the form of entertainment is involved.

THE BOARDS

Over a century ago, the sport of motorcycle racing began. The Hendee Mfg. Co. introduced the Indian in 1901 and was followed by Harley Davidson in 1903. Racing them ensued shortly thereafter, on horse tracks and bicycle velodromes. Special high-banked board tracks became the big deal, with one being built in Beverly Hills, where the Beverly Wilshire Hotel stands today. The high cost of maintenance ended this interesting concept several years later. Those races were very dangerous and many riders lost their lives, along with spectators who would stand alongside the crash walls for a better view. All of this evolved into the AMA racing group that is still in existence today.

I remember seeing the likes of Skip Van Leeuwen, and Sammy "The Flying Flea" Tanner roaring around the dirt tracks, thrilling fans with every daring move. Tonight, you will get to see this unique form of racing, featuring today's stars in action on our little short track. Should you like to see some of the history up close, I recommend that you visit the Solvang Vintage Motorcycle Museum. You can get information at www.motosolvang.com. They have a Thor board track racer from 1913 on display, along with many other historic bikes and memorabilia. Now, sit back and enjoy our night of AMA racing, it should be a good one.

SOMETHING IS WRONG

Remember back when you hustled out on Thursday nights to watch the mighty Midgets run here at Ventura Raceway. Or, maybe you were one of those Tuesday night Speedway bike fans. Times have certainly changed in our world, over these past many years, since those glory days. What would it take to get you here on a week night in today's world? Remember, everything is faster today. You were supposed to have plenty of free time, what with all of the great time-saving devices that have been invented in the last twenty years. The futurists were predicting that you would be living a life of leisure with more free time than you could spend.

Something must have gone wrong, as it seems that the predictions of the leisure life have not panned out as predicted. People today are on a very fast treadmill that never seems to slow down. Most people I know are working more hours than ever before, and have less free time to spend. Their phones and cars travel at light speed in comparison to yesterday. Back in the day, if you broke a part on your race car you had to make a new one. Today, you pick up your iPhone and FedEx delivers it to you in the morning. Maybe I am old fashioned and can be accused of living in the past, but something is wrong with this high tech life we are living.

HAPPY DAYS

Last weekend, at the Ventura Fairgrounds, and all over downtown, they held the Nationals. A weekend of music, cars, and the Fonz. It is interesting to watch the different groupings of people who attend this event. They are comprised of young people dressed up in outfits that were in vogue during the '50s and another group of older folks, who actually did grow up in the '50s. The younger set wishing they could have, and the older set reliving their memories, with cars they may have owned, or wished they had owned, when they grew up during that era.

Having grown up in the '50s, and having owned a couple of those cars made it fun to look back and remember how simple times were during that era. Your wardrobe consisted of Levi's, white t-shirts, and a windbreaker. Getting dressed up would consist of cords and a bowling shirt or something to that effect. One thing you did not see much of back then were tattoos. They were mostly seen on Navy guys from the local military bases. Today, the human body has become a walking art pallet. It will be interesting to watch all of that art sag as the wearer's age into middle age and beyond. Just the thought of it can be kind of scary.

Racing back in that era was also very simplistic, what with race teams building their own stuff. The age of computers and all of the high tech gadgetry we see today has changed the racing world. It would be great if there was an event that gathered all of the old timer's and their cars together in one spot. The young fans and racers of today could wish they had been there to experience the era, and the old folks could tell the stories of that bygone era.

THE GOLD CUP

I just returned from my annual trip to the Gold Cup Race of Champions at the Silver Dollar Speedway in Chico. Having started in 1951, this event was celebrating its 60th anniversary. It all began at Hughes Stadium in Sacramento and was won by John Soares, who is the current promoter at Antioch and Merced. It then moved to West Capital Raceway and then to Chico in 1980. The cars that raced in this event evolved from the Jalopies to Modifieds and then to Sprint Cars. It is still evolving, as this year it featured Midgets, and traditional wingless Sprint Cars on Thursday night. The World of Outlaws are featured on Friday and Saturday nights and they put on a great show against the locals. The locals put forth an even greater show, taking the first five positions and all of the cash.

This long-standing tradition is good for racing, and they had a Hall of Fame set up with drivers and cars from every era. Steve Kinser has dominated this event over the years with 12 wins from 1978 to 2005. Even though his dominance has faded, the memories still remain. Consider that the next driver on the all-times list is Jac Haudenschild, with three victories. The long history of this event continues to draw big crowds and every top Sprint Car driver currently running today. I highly recommend that you add this one to your bucket list. The racing on this fast ¼ mile is some of the best around, and the tradition of the Gold Cup adds the glamour. Don't miss the next one, you won't regret it.

STATE OF THE UNION

As the season winds down, it is time to reflect on what the year has brought. It is also time to project what the future of our sport looks like in the years ahead. All of us tend to look back and reflect about the "good old days" and how great they were. Well guess what! These are the "good old days," especially to those young enough to have not been around when car counts and fan attendance were much higher than today.

With the exception of big events like Knoxville, the Chili Bowl, Indiana Speed Week, the Gold Cup, and the Trophy Cup, weekly attendance is off and car counts are down all across the country. The racing industry is facing very difficult times, what with an economy that has tanked, and the future not too bright. The cost of running a race team has sky rocketed to a point where the average person can no longer afford to participate. This has put a huge dent in car counts at most levels of the racing world. Even major teams like John Force have lost the sponsorship of Castrol and Ford. This will be a heavy blow to Drag Racing and racing in general.

As fans, we need to stick out the economic downturn and support our local tracks as much as possible. If we don't, there won't be any good old days for the next generation to talk about. Think about it. If local racing around the country were to cease, it would never return. Saturday night would become the "Loneliest Night of the Year." It would however, be a good song title.

BIG DEAL

I am heading out for Tulare for another running of the Trophy Cup. This event has been held for many years, and this year's event is the 20th annual. A big part of its success is due to the fact that the local towns and business entities all get behind the event. The benefactor of this event is "Make-A-Wish." For many years, the dollar figure raised has increased to around $200,000 and growing each year. The Trophy Cup is now a three night event with non-wing cars competing on Thursday night and the wing show on Friday and Saturday night. The car count for the wing show is 96, with drivers from all over the country competing for the Cup. That car count is only 20 less than the Knoxville Nationals, which tells you something about the impact of this long-running event.

It makes you wonder about the differences between them and us. Down here in the south, we are like poor cousins who have been left out in the cold. Having a major three-day event is next to impossible. Traffic jams are now the order of the day and getting anywhere has now become a nightmare. There are only two venues left that feature open wheel racing. Here at Ventura and Perris, both tracks suffer from bad traffic syndrome, making multi-day events next to impossible to promote. Once upon a time, we had the Turkey Night race at Ascot. It has bounced around and is now at Perris for its one-night show. The Oval Nationals continues to try for a three-nighter, but only gets a decent crowd on Saturday. Maybe those small towns in the valley have an advantage with actual open space for miles between them. Makes sense to me!

GONE

They say that nothing lasts forever, and I would have to agree. Nothing, in this case, is my favorite music venue, Zoey's Café. It closed its doors last week, after quite a few years of presenting an alternative music venue. Steve and his wife, Polly, labored endlessly to bring the locals the music they claimed to love. If you mentioned Zoey's, everyone would rave about what they provided for the city. But did they love it enough? Not really, because if they did, they would have supported it on a regular basis, sponsored artists or special shows.

People talk a lot of their love for the arts, just as people talk a lot about their love of Sprint Car and Midget Car racing. But do they really love it enough to get behind it and make it work. We lost two Southern California Sprint Car venues recently. Victorville and San Bernardino closed their doors and it is doubtful they will reopen anytime soon. This leaves just two venues in Southern California to carry the torch for the so called "Lovers of Open Wheel Racing Groupies" to follow their sport. This is the same group that complains about a $15 admission fee and having to pay for parking. All of this goes on while some track operator and his crew spend endless hours trying to make the show a good one. Like Steve and Polly, their days are numbered. Time is running out for this merry band of open wheel fans. Economics and lifestyles of today's younger crowd won't be enough to make it pay. The world has changed and not necessarily for the better. How many carnivals and circus shows have you seen setting up in the neighborhood lately? No matter how much you love something, economics rule the world of business. Just loving something will not keep the door open.

Ventura Raceway Articles

2014

BACK AT IT!

Sometimes, it seems as though we just finished a season, and here it is time to start again. Of course, racing has become a year-round deal, as it starts the first weekend in January and ends on Thanksgiving weekend. This year started with the Chili Bowl, and that event has become a giant homecoming for race fans around the world. They come out of the woodwork to be a part of what has become the "Woodstock" of racing. I must admit, with 280 Midget cars and five great nights of racing, it is something to behold and not to be missed.

Another thing not to be missed is the last full-time season with the World of Outlaws for Steve "The King" Kinser. After some thirty years and well over 500 main event wins, he will hang up (for the most part), his active racing career. No longer will he be racing in every dirt track across the country, as he has all of these years. This is his farewell tour and if you have never had the opportunity, you should not miss him on the upcoming Outlaw tour. Best bet is to catch him at the Tulare Thunderbowl, on Friday and Saturday night, March 14/15. It will be a great show and Ventura Raceway is dark, so make the journey north and take in some winged racing with the Outlaws and Steve Kinser. Winged Sprint Cars will also be a part of the schedule here in Ventura on September 13...This will be a big event and a lot of my friends from the north are already making plans to visit Ventura, many for the first time, when the King of the West 410s visit us. I think this will be the first time for winged Sprint Cars at this facility. I can't wait to see them here at the beach.

Welcome to opening night for all of the classes here at the Raceway, and have a great time.

END OF AN ERA

The big rigs pulled into Tulare for the World of Outlaws two-night show. Race rigs and souvenir trailers set up for the big show as the fans start to gather in the camp grounds and the parking lot. There is an electric feeling, as the talk is all about the farewell tour of the "KING." Steve Kinser is making his final full season tour with the Outlaws. He helped build the series over the last thirty some-odd years. He is a twenty time champion of the series. This is a record that I doubt will ever be matched. Today's racing world is more even, due to everyone having the same high tech equipment off the shelf. Back in the day, Steve fought with Doug Wolfgang, Bobby Allen, Jan Opperman, Sammy Swindell and others for titles he won handily. It was a pure driver and crew chief combination that many times made the difference between winning and losing. As good as the competition was, no one could match his ability behind the wheel coupled with Karl Kinser working the set up. So, he is back for one last run at a title. Let's hope he can bring it home, as it would be a great good-bye to go out a champion one more time.

The Outlaws continue their west coast swing and then will head back east in their almost endless pursuit of putting on the "Greatest Show on Dirt." It truly lives up to the hype, as the crowds are big and the excitement of the "Outlaw Circus" rivals that of Ringling Brothers. USAC shared the show on Friday night and put on a great main event. However, their lack of marketing leaves so much to be desired, it is laughable. Too bad, because the sport of Sprint Car racing needs more than one "Really Big Show."

SPACE

Space is something we all relish and try to protect at all costs. Just look out on the track and you will see the drivers fighting for space in order to finish in the front of the pack. Invade their space and they will knock you off the pace in order to get that all-important win. They can and do justify their actions on the track, in order to win the glory that goes along with a victory.

I have found, that for the most part, people think and act like their time and space is more important than any other person. You can see it every day, as drivers never give other drivers a wave-over or a go-ahead. They just crowd and push their way around the world because of a bloated ego, and inflated thoughts of self-importance. Oh, sometimes they will give out a single digit salute about your being number one, but even that is ego driven.

Today, we spent the afternoon at the Santa Barbara Museum of Art. They have a photo exhibit entitled, "Heavenly Bodies." Sorry guys, it is not the S.I. swimsuit issue. On display are some of the most incredible space pictures you will ever see. The expanse of the endless universe and beyond is spellbinding, to say the least. As I stood there taking it all in, I realized that we are just a tiny speck of dust in a vast system that is so mammoth you cannot envision it in your mind. So, next time you get the urge to crowd out someone in line or making a lane change, give them a wave instead. None of us specs of dust, need to be in that big of a hurry. Of course, if you are on the track and battling for the lead, you need not follow this suggestion.

SPECIAL EVENTS

I happen to enjoy special events, especially in the world of auto racing. They have an energy level that is missing from a normal weekly show. Not that the weekly shows are not good, in fact, sometimes they can be better than the special events. However, the special events tend to gather the same fan base each year. This builds an event over the years and makes it special. The race fans look forward to seeing other people they met, and became friends with, from other parts of the country. Some of my favorite special events are the Gold Cup in Chico, the Trophy Cup in Tulare, the Knoxville Nationals, and the grand daddy of them all, the Chili Bowl.

The Chili Bowl has grown to be the biggest of any special event and prides itself in this role. Fans travel from all over the world each and every year to re-connect with friends at this very special venue. This success has also had a downside on the sport of Midget racing. The Bowl attracts around 280 cars and drivers, along with their teams. The cost of running the Chili Bowl is very high, as travel expenses for more than a week on the road add up in a hurry. I can't help but think that this huge expense, stops a lot of smaller teams from running much else, for the rest of the year. Therefore, a big percentage of those 280 cars may only run the Bowl. This hurts the weekly shows all over the country. It certainly showed the trend here for our Midgets.

I certainly hope that our special events get a lot of support. We will have the 410 USAC Sprints, the King of the West Wing Sprinters, the AMA Speedway Bikes, all coming to town this season. And, our Battle at the Beach should be considered a special event. If the drivers and fans support this four-race series, it, too, could become truly special. Let's hope so.

WHO'S GONNA FILL THEIR SHOES

Legendary country singer George Jones had a hit back in 1985 titled "Who's Gonna Fill Their Shoes." The lyrics tell about all of the great original country singers who pioneered the music from the beginning until today. Hank Williams, Marty Robbins, Elvis and Patsy Cline are a few of the stars he sings about. A few are still around, like Willie Nelson and Merle Haggard, but they are disappearing fast, as time waits for no one. His song and video tell about those who lived a lifetime, pursuing their craft of music and were able to become the stars of country music. You can catch his video on Google by looking up "Who's Gonna Fill Their Shoes-George Jones."

The fact that makes the video interesting is that it is filmed in a gas station that has been passed over by an interstate highway. Much like those that faded away on Route 66, when Interstate 40 bypassed the old highway. They were replaced by a new generation of truck stops and rest stops. Big corporate travel centers now dot the highways and cars travel at much higher rates of speed in their quest to save time. Gone are the days of personal service by an independent operator of a "filling station." I have found a few along the Interstates, but they are a rarity.

All of us, who have been around awhile, are much like those filling stations of yesteryear. We will be gone before you know it and a new lifestyle will take our place. We recently lost one of the best of the "old school guys": Dave Wolfe, the guy in orange, you would see out in the infield taking pictures of the racers and around the pit area with his wagon full of the photographs. Dave always had a good joke or story about what was happening around the race track. His personality filled our world with laughter, and his smile was always a welcome sight. So, who will fill his shoes?? Hopefully, another interesting person will come along with good jokes, super photos and fun stories. Or, will it be a flying drone and people taking selfies that become the rest stops on tomorrow's interstate of life…let's hope not.

PLACE YOUR BETS

In spite of the fact that Sprint Car racing is one of the most exciting sports one can watch, the number of fans in the stands seems to stay the same. How do we expose this great sport to new fans is the question that is always raised when serious discussions on the sport take place.

I think I have the answer: Pari-mutuel betting on the races! Just imagine, lines of people at the betting windows placing their bets on their favorite driver. This takes place on horse racing every day just a few hundred yards from Ventura Raceway. Horse tracks across the country are hooked up via satellite, where bettors can place bets on the various events being held. A portion of the wagers go to the various tracks, which in turn makes for larger purses for the winning riders and owners.

Just imagine the crowds this would draw to the races, and all of the excitement this new format would bring to our sport. The morning line odds would be published based on past driver performance, and race analysts would be touting their "picks" for the night's events. Fans across the country would be placing their bets. A whole new industry would be established and thus would bring "big bucks" into the purse structure. This would enable more cars, and thus more fans into the stands. Sound crazy? Not really, at least in my mind. Of course, my mind is always thinking outside the box, so it makes sense to me, you can bet on it.

THE BIG ONE

"The Month of May"—I remember when it was the biggest month of the year culminating in the running of the "Big One" at the Indianapolis Motor Speedway on Memorial Day. I couldn't wait to hear it on the radio with Sid Collins calling all of the action in such a way that one could picture in their mind the actual event as it unfolded.

Then a miracle of modern science was introduced with closed circuit broadcasting of the race. My father and I went down to see the race live at the Olympic Auditorium in living black and white. There it was on a giant screen for all to see . . . what a sight!

So much has changed over the years. Now you can watch it on your own big screen TV in the comfort of your home in full color and with surround sound. Those great radio commentators with their descriptive insights are gone. Today's broadcasters do not have the same descriptive powers of those legends of yesteryear. I hate to sound like a "remember the good old days" person, however, it just doesn't seem as good as it used to be.

Thirty-three cars "maybe," all identical, with 33 motors, basically all identical, just doesn't compare with the times of the past when teams showed up with "their" concept of what would be the fastest car to last the 500 miles and win the "big one." Technology has eliminated all of that and the event is sadly lacking in excitement for that reason. This, along with politically correct drivers and their corporate sponsorships, leaves the event and the league lacking in excitement. Of course, we will all watch. After all, it is the "big one."

MAJOR EVENTS

Major events seem to dominate the scene in all forms of racing. This, in turn, has a negative effect on weekly shows throughout the land. The Indy 500 dominates the IRL with its massive crowds and TV coverage. If you look at the other IRL shows, you will find empty seats and not a lot of big TV build-up prior to the event. It seems as though we have been brain-washed, and we suffer from some "Big Event" Psycho Syndrome affliction. This is not exclusive to auto racing. Horse racing suffers from the same malady. California Chrome will be running for the Triple Crown, an almost impossible feat to accomplish. This horse is part of one of the great sporting stories of all time. A plain Jane horse with no highbrow breeding, owned by Average Joe owners, and a trainer who is older than dirt. Together, they may just pull off the Triple Crown, and go down in history in a sport that needs this to happen. You see, horse racing also suffers from "Big Event" Psycho Syndrome. The Kentucky Derby and the other two legs of the Triple Crown have record crowds each year. However, most horse race tracks are suffering from dismal attendance from fans, who for many reasons are just not taking in the weekly shows. There are many reasons for this. Times change, people change, habits change. Change is everywhere and it won't stop soon. The future will include more special events and less weekly stuff, as the reality of economics continues to rule the world in which we live. Besides, someday most everything could end up in a virtual reality world, in which you never leave your house. I'm glad I won't be around to witness that one.

GREEN, WHITE, CHECKER

Watching the Indy 500 this year was rather interesting. Speeds have increased to around 230 mph. The last time this happened, they invoked rules so the cars would slow down. They feared the higher speeds would result in catastrophic accidents and possible injuries or worse. This year, they celebrated the higher speed runs with joyful cheerleading by the announcing team. So what are we to believe? Are the new higher speeds truly safer due to higher technology? Or, are they just ignoring the safety factors and hoping for the best? Only time will tell. Another factor that made the race exciting was the red flag just before the finish after an accident would have resulted in a yellow flag finish. This would have been a real bummer had they not stopped the action to clean up the debris. Racing needs a green flag finish, especially the Indy 500. The fans were treated to a dazzling final lap showdown that could have been won by either driver.

Who knows what the future will bring to Indy Car. They had 33 cars for the event but only 21 the following race. This seems to be the case with all of motorsports and is something that is a major concern throughout the country. Car counts are the topic of discussion wherever you go in the racing world. I guess we might as well get used to it, as I see no solution in the near future. Just enjoy what we have and keep coming back. What is, is.

STEP UP TO THE PLATE

If you look at the state of the union in racing today, it is a pretty complex situation to really understand what is going on. Like the national economy, one can see highlights, like a record stock market and think everything is great. However, when you look at the real world, the details don't seem to make sense as less people are in the actual work force. NASCAR is still big on television, but they are tearing out thousands of seats in every stadium across the nation due to lack of fans. I remember my trip back to the Indy 500 many years ago. One of the highlights was the night before the 500 Midget Race, at Raceway Park. Thirty-three Midgets lined up in 11 rows of three for what was a superb event on this very fast racetrack. I am told that there were three rows of three for a total of nine cars at this year's event. This is a sad fact of life, especially for Midget and Sprint Car fans across the country. Face it, car counts are not coming back any time soon. We, the fans, must face this reality and get used to it. Like I said last week, what is, is! We, the fans need to support our local short tracks and the sport, if it is to survive this economy and survive for the future. One way is to attend races as much as possible, and the other is to support the sport in any way possible. Do you subscribe to the publications that cover the sport? *National Speed Sport News*, *Sprint Car and Midget Magazine*, and *Flat-Out Magazine* are three terrific publications that really cover the racing world. If you are a true fan of Midget and Sprint Car racing, along with racing in general, then you should be a subscriber to these three publications. I know you can get free info on the internet very quickly. However, these three publications are the heartbeat of our racing world. Support them if you want your racing world to grow in the future.

HISTORY LESSON

I spent last Saturday morning at the Mullen Automotive Museum in Oxnard. This is one great display of historic automobiles. The museum currently features a vast array of the legendary Bugatti cars, along with art and furniture created by the Bugatti family. The Bugatti cars were very prominent in racing for many decades and led the sport in technological advancement. This, along with luxury street versions of the famous brand, created one of the greatest automotive legacies in the history of the industry. The museum is only open two days a month so if you want to visit, check them out at www.mullinautomotivemuseum. com. Don't miss this.

Next stop for me is the Knoxville Nationals and my annual visit to the National Sprint Car Hall of Fame. Their feature display this year is the Steve Kinser cars. Steve Kinser's career has lasted 40 years. Kinser ruled the World of Outlaws and ran up 577 main event wins, a record that will probably never be broken. Kinser will be remembered as the "King of the Outlaws." If you are a history buff and love Sprint Car racing, it would behoove you to join the National Sprint Car Hall of Fame. They are currently raising funds to add display space and could use your (yes, that is you) support by joining this great organization. Their mission is to preserve the history of our sport. If you call yourself a Sprint Car fan then how about it…send in a donation for the cause. Their website is www.sprintcarhof.com.

KING OF THE HILL

I just returned from the Knoxville Nationals. As always, it was a great trip. The National Sprint Car Hall of Fame had an incredible salute to Steve Kinser. Seven of his historic cars were featured, spanning a forty-year career. Kinser's stats are legendary. As a fan of Sprint Car racing, you will be impressed at the dominance one driver could generate over time. Sprint Car racing's ultimate prize is winning the Knoxville Nationals, and only a few have won it more than once. Kinser has won 12 of them over his career, which is more than anyone else. He was truly "King of the Hill" for many years. Alas, time marches on, and history shows that the king is always dethroned by a younger, more powerful opponent. "Long Live the King," is the fans mantra, until he starts to show signs of age and weakness. In this case, the new upstart is Donnie Schatz, who has now won eight of the last nine nationals. No one seems to be able to match his ability with a Sprint Car. Schatz is both loved and hated by the fans, which is a normal thing. He is dethroning a legend and huge fan favorite in Steve Kinser. Steve will step aside after this season. As Arnold Palmer stepped aside for Jack Nicklaus, the cycle of life continues. What that means for Steve, only Steve will know. Stepping down from your life passion is a very difficult transition in life. If you were lucky enough to follow your life passion, then you will understand.

DIRT TRACK DILEMMA

History seems to repeat itself in spite of hard lessons learned over time. It was just announced that a group of drivers are leaving the All Stars Sprint Car series and forming a new group called the Renegade Sprints. I guess they think they have all the answers to how a series should be run. Two series in a small region of the country will not work. Looking back at similar situations should have given them some insight into the pitfalls of this sort of action. In 1989, the USA series was created and failed in its attempt to outdo the Outlaws. In 2005, the National Sprint Series attempted to do the same, with the Outlaws once again winning out. The Outlaws still hold court over the 410 Sprint Car world nationwide and will more than likely continue to do so as long as there are enough cars and fans to make it work. In our own region, we had the big battle between the SCRA and USAC, with USAC winning out. The questions is, was it truly a win? Most of us would agree, that it destroyed what was once a solid group, that has never been the same since. Just a short time ago, another group of discontented drivers managed to split up the 360 Sprint Car series in California. This is still an ongoing situation with neither side really winning, as car counts aren't what they should be at any venue. So time marches on to the beat of the same old drum . . . Big egos never really make for better racing, and in time it will all come to an end, with no one winning the battle . . . but everyone losing the war.

MARGARITAVILLE

Big events seem to be the order of the day in our racing world. This year, I have attended the Chili Bowl, the World of Outlaws at Tulare, the Knoxville Nationals, and the Gold Cup at Chico. What makes these events so special is the fact that they only happen once a year. Every event had one thing in common, very large sold-out crowds of race fans, who don't care what the price is, because for each of them, it is a must-attend happening. These events have become an annual reunion of race friends who may only see each other once a year. They converge on these venues like a group of "Parrot Heads" to see Jimmy Buffett & the Coral Reefer Band. They have a common bond amongst each other that is based around Sprint Car racing, like the "Parrot Heads" have for Jimmy Buffett's music. In the case of Sprint Car racing, they are referred to as "Thunderheads," which is of course, the concept I used while producing my line of race wear. This is all great, and the events themselves are really a lot of fun to attend. I, of course, will have them all on my schedule for next year, as I am a Thunderhead. Myself, like all of Jimmy's Parrot Heads, really have a blast with all of our good friends at these events. The only problem I foresee in the future is that these fans are not attending the smaller shows at their local venues. Car counts and crowd counts are down nationwide at most weekly shows, as fans are spending their money on the big shows. This creates a double-edged sword, with a soon-to-be lack of cars even at the big events. An example of this is the Knoxville Nationals which used to draw around 150 cars and now the number is down to 100. As fans, if we do not support the weekly shows, we will also see the big events dwindle. The music industry faces the same dilemma, as small music venues can't make it in today's world. Where will the next Jimmy Buffett or Steve Kinser come from in tomorrow's world? Give it some thought!

CIVIL WAR

The Winged Sprint Cars of the King of the West series, ventured down from Northern California recently, for what was a great evening of racing here in Ventura. I have been a fan of the wing-style Sprint Cars for many years. I have made many a trip up north, and to the Knoxville Nationals, to watch them battle it out in their form of Sprint Car racing. Of course, most all of my Southern California friends mocked this form of racing, and stood firm in their belief that only traditional Sprint Cars were worth watching. I think we can all agree, that they put on a great show at our facility, and I hope that they will return again next year. It would be even better, if it was a 360 show, and that our guys would put wings on their cars. This would create a duel that could be titled "The Civil War Sprint Car Championship." North verses the South, in a shootout featuring two nights of racing. Friday night would be a traditional non-wing show and Saturday night would be a wing event. Just imagine, what an exciting weekend of racing it would be. They have plenty of drivers that can run with or without wings. Bud Keading and Andy Forsberg are just two of their guys that come to mind, who can run both styles with skill and are real racers, who put on a show in either style of car. Greg Taylor showed that our guys can also run with a wing on their cars. This would make for a very interesting evening.

Other features of this event, that I think we should adapt at our track, are the four-wide salute lap and the double file restarts. These two items add drama to the evening and make for an interesting program. In addition, there were a lot of fans who made the long journey down to our track for the first time. They were really impressed with the location on the beach and loved the racing action. If you noticed, they also stayed after the main event to salute the drivers and listen to the interviews. This is something that always happens up north and becomes an after-race celebration that would be nice to see our own fans duplicate.

THE CHILI BOWL

CHILI BOWL ARTICLES

The Thunderhead line of racing apparel made its first appearance at the 1996 Chili Bowl Nationals. That is the event where I introduced Thunderhead Racing Apparel. The concept was for a more sophisticated look for race fans. In essence, I wanted the Thunderhead experience to be different, more a state of mind. The concept was well received and Thunderhead was on its way.

Being a part of the Chili Bowl has been a very enriching experience. Over all of these years, Emmett, Lanny, Donna, and the terrific staff at the Chili Bowl have treated me like family. I cannot find the words to express my appreciation for what this has meant to me. Thank you to all of them and much success in the future of this great event.

In 2006, I began to write articles for the Chili Bowl program. This proved to be a challenge. However, the larger format allowed me more space to expand the thought process. The nine articles have evolved over the years into what I believe are very interesting themes. The writing experience of this series has been a pleasure. I hope you enjoy them.

THUNDERTALK
TOM "THUNDERHEAD" TOUTZ

THE GREATEST
SPECTACLE IN RACING

I remember way back when I was a kid and the INDY 500 was considered to be the "greatest spectacle in racing." I would look forward each spring to being able to listen to the great Sid Collins describe the event over the radio.

It was spectacular to hear his commentary. It made me feel as though I was there. Eventually, I made it to Indy. To actually be there and witness the biggest event in racing, was a dream come true. Of course, it didn't happen until I was 50 years old, and by then the event had lost some of its luster. Today, the Indy 500, has lost most of its allure to the American open wheel race fan. We all know the reasons for this, so I will not delve into them.

Today, we have the "greatest spectacle in racing" in a different form. It is called the "Chili Bowl." I first came to this event in 1996 and have been coming ever since. Now, I look forward each year to being part of an event which has grown in stature, to the point of being a "not miss" event. The greatest drivers from all over the country gather once a year, and the fans get to witness the best racing action anywhere. In my opinion, nothing compares to Midgets on a Bull Ring. Non-stop, from Tuesday through Saturday, 250+ cars, all vying for the honor of being a "Chili Bowl Champion." It has become a true gathering of the racing fans, where one can see the very best from racing divisions far and wide. A true spectacle to behold.

Who would have guessed that twenty years ago, when Emmett Hahn and Lanny Edwards threw the dice, that their little event would become the monster hit it is today. A true "Field of Dreams" for both race fans and drivers. Once a year, in the most unlikely of places…indoors… Tulsa…dead of winter…go figure. It is truly the "greatest spectacle in racing."

THUNDERTALK
TOM "THUNDERHEAD" TOUTZ
ROAD TRIP

Can you believe it? It is Chili Bowl time again! It seems as though we were anticipating the first race of the season only yesterday. Now comes mid-winter and it is time for my annual pilgrimage to Mecca. Mecca to Midget Car race fans is the Chili Bowl Nationals in Tulsa, Oklahoma. No doubt about it, the biggest event, on any race fans schedule.

Three days on the road can seem long to some folks, but, I really enjoy the journey. It is filled with anticipation of the great racing ahead, and also in meeting up with old friends, some of which I only get to see at the Chili Bowl.

As the miles roll on, it gives me time to reflect on the past, and plan for the future, without the phone ringing every ten minutes at the office. It is also a time to turn the van into a rolling concert venue and listen to some great road music as the miles pass by. My musical tastes run the gamut from country to classical, and most everything in between. Here are some of my favorite road songs and artists that help the time pass: Hot Rod Lincoln, Truck Drivin' Man, Lookin' at the World Through a Windshield, Momma Hated Diesels, Seeds and Stems, all by Commander Cody and the Lost Planet Airmen. Of course, anything by Willie Nelson, Merle Haggard, Buck Owens, George Jones, Ernest Tubb, Gillian Welch, Jimmie Dale Gilmore, Kinky Friedman, Johnny Cash, Dwight Yokum, and Hank Williams round out the country portion of the concert. Assorted CD's with Bill Monroe, The Nitty Gritty Dirt Band, and Split Lip Rayfield, fill the blue grass category. I have the complete library of rhythm and blues from 1956-1968. This, along with great jazz, from Eddie "Clean Head" Vinson, Etta James, Miles Davis, and John Coltrane, coupled with some Mozart and Vivaldi, round out my musical preferences. They make for quite a concert rolling down Interstate 40.

The best part of any journey is the anticipation. Think back to your last vacation. You talked about it, and thought about it for many weeks before you left. Just like this years Chili Bowl. You have been talking about it, and looking forward to it since last year. Now you are here, the fun begins, and the time will fly by like a flash, as it always does, when you are having a great time. There is nothing like being at the Chili Bowl! Anyone back home, who didn't make the pilgrimage, are eating their hearts out!

THUNDERTALK
TOM "THUNDERHEAD" TOUTZ
HEROES

Webster's Dictionary defines hero as "A man (or woman) celebrated for special achievements and attributes."

I bought the latest Dwight Yokum CD the other day. It is titled "Dwight Sings Buck" and is a tribute Yokum's hero, Buck Owens. Buck was a classic country singer, who influenced Yokum's development as an artist. Together, back in 1989, they had a hit song titled, "Streets of Bakersfield." I watched them perform it at a concert at Universal. Quite a show it was, and the hero persona was evident in the performance.

Each of us has had heroes, throughout our life, and the racing world is full of them. A few of my heroes early on were Parnelli Jones, Sterling Moss, Ken Miles, Mario Andretti, and A.J. Foyt. This type of hero is a figment of our imagination. We don't know them personally, so our only connection is that of press clippings, and seeing them perform. We base our opinion of them, on their achievements in a sport, not on really knowing them up close and personal. If we knew them up close, they may appear to be somewhat tarnished from their public persona, then again, maybe not.

I do remember one hero of mine from my slalom racing days. His name was "Pop" Price, the father of two of my competitors. He was always there with advice and encouragement, even though I was trying to beat his kids at the races. There was something special about his outlook on life that I still feel today. An unsung hero, maybe, but not to me. These are the true heroes in our lives, the unsung ones. Have you been one lately?

THUNDERTALK
TOM "THUNDERHEAD" TOUTZ
LOW BUCK RACER

Racing for the pure love of the sport is the low buck contender. He is seen at every race. His passion keeps him coming back, as he works to find parts and sponsorships.

Ventura Raceway recently had such a racer. Brandon Thomson, a young, passionate Sprint Car enthusiast, along with his dad and grandfather, showed up each week and gave it their all. While not having top-notch equipment, they still had to compete against well-funded teams. The fans continued each week rooting for them, looking forward to the day Brandon would be the top low buck racer.

The last race at Ventura Raceway offered $5,000 to win. I asked Brandon before the race what he had planned to do to win the race. He stated with confidence, that he would run the bottom and force the other racers to run the top. He stated that the top would go away in the last ten laps, giving him a shot at the big prize. Serious competition was facing him with Cory Kruseman, Jesse "The Rocket" Hockett, Jonathan Henry and twenty other big money cars starting behind him.

Brandon was on the pole for the main event. His plan seemed to be working until a yellow flag gave the big guns the chance to out horsepower him on the re-start. He continued his plan by staying on the bottom, running them down in the last ten laps to take the checkered flag and the $5,000. The crowd went wild. What a victory for a deserving young man! This was a dream for Brandon, his first main event win at Ventura Raceway.

What does this have to do with the Chili Bowl? Every year, I come here hoping to see a low buck team win this event. The Chili Bowl has become the most prestigious racing event of the year. Every big name driver is here with the latest trick equipment and big money. It is time to see a Brandon in the winner's circle holding up the trophy of victory.

THUNDERTALK
TOM "THUNDERHEAD" TOUTZ
WORLD SERIES

The year was 1946 and the country was fixated on Midget Car racing. From the west coast to the east coast, huge crowds were filling race tracks to the maximum.

Not just on Saturday night, but four and five nights a week, the Midgets were the toast of the town. In California, where I am from, there were two circuits, the Red and the Blue doing battle at such venues as the Coliseum, the Rose Bowl, Gilmore Stadium and many others. The Coliseum and the Rose Bowl are still part of Southern California, but the Midgets have long gone from those major venues and the glory days of that era. However, we still have a loyal group, small though it is, of fans and drivers that follow, and participate in the sport. Ventura Raceway ended the season with the J.W. Mitchell Fall Classic during Thanksgiving week. Forty-six Midget cars and a nice crowd were thrilled with great racing action. Brad Kuhn came in from the Midwest and stole the show and the $5,000 winner's purse. This pales in comparison with the winner of the 1946 Midget race at the Coliseum where 60,000 fans watched the winner walk away with $8,000. Based on inflation, Brads winning prize should have been at least $100,000 or more. The cost of racing a Midget is off-the-charts, with a motor costing in the neighborhood of $35-$50,000. What is wrong with this picture?

What happened to cause the demise of this great sport? The answer to that can be very complicated, and many theories prevail. One theory is as follows. This is a big country, and Midget racing was fragmented on a regional basis. AAA, and many other groups sanctioned Midget racing from coast to coast. The problem with this is that there was no national circuit, ending with a World Series, or a Super Bowl. The National Football League, Major League Baseball and the NBA accomplished this format, and became the big leagues of sport during the 1950s and 1960s. They expanded coast to coast and became the dominant sport for people to go and see. Had Midget racing formed a national league with a World Series type finish, perhaps it would still be a major league sport today. USAC had a chance to accomplish this when they were formed after AAA left the scene. The organization, United States Auto Club, was, and still is, a Midwest deal. Yes, we have the Western States Midgets, but, they are truly, a stepchild of USAC.

During this same period, NASCAR expanded nationwide and became the top dog of racing in this country.

Alas, it is what it is! The Chili Bowl is now the World Series of Midget racing. Each year we gather together, both fans and drivers, in Tulsa, for this major event. With a car count pushing 300, I can only guess that every Midget in this country will make it here to Tulsa, and compete for the Driller Trophy. The money is irrelevant, as it is in all of Midget racing across the country. Midget racing is a lot like Polo in that respect, with the cost of a horse far in excess of common sense. So, let's once again throw common sense to the wind, and enjoy this great week in Tulsa.

THUNDERTALK
TOM "THUNDERHEAD" TOUTZ

THE CROSSROADS

Midget racing was born in the mid thirties during the depths of the great depression. Somehow, it managed to survive even under those most drastic of economic times. World War II interrupted the racing world from 1941 to 1945. At the conclusion of the war, Midget racing bounced back, bigger than ever, to become one of our nations leading sports series. Coast to coast, fans packed stadiums, to watch the Mighty Midgets do battle. Traveling series of drivers and teams thrilled audiences several nights a week. Then, for many reasons, their popularity dwindled, and only the purist drivers and fans were left to follow the sport. We are those fortunate ones, following the sport to this day.

Today, we find ourselves in another economic downfall, as our economy has tanked and the cost of both driving in, and attending races, has skyrocketed. We can blame the economy. However, we also need to look at why Midget racing is so expensive. Yes, we are to blame for much of the rising costs. Midget motors run $40,000, and you need several variations for short track and big track use. This insanity has to stop.

We now find ourselves at a crossroad, and I, for one, hope we choose the right path. The future of Midget racing is now! Part of what makes our sport so great is the diversity of engines that are used. Along with many chassis options, this makes it the absolute best of any racing series running today. No cookie cutter creations or spec cars to dull the action on the track. There is a lot of talk going around about this subject, and I hope a solution is found that allows the cost of racing to drop. The future of the sport is on the line, and must be dealt with in order to survive.

The Chili Bowl is probably the main reason that Midget racing is still around today. For whatever reason, and there are many, this event has revived the sport, and has taken it to a new level. The car count probably includes every Midget in the country and every driver and fan I talk to wants to be part of the show. At my home track, Ventura Raceway, we will be having a VRA Midget series in 2011. They are working on a cost reduction setup that will allow a team to operate, on a reasonable budget. This became a reality, because many of the drivers built a car, just to run in the Chili Bowl.

Like I said, we stand at the crossroads. Let's hope the decisions made for the future will enable the sport to survive and prosper. Not just at the Chili Bowl, but across the country.

THUNDERTALK
TOM "THUNDERHEAD" TOUTZ
LOST HIGHWAY

Route 66 opened up the west for travel to everyone in the midwest and beyond. It winds from Chicago to L.A., right through the heart of Tulsa. Along with it came towns and businesses that thrived, due to the travelers that used the road. The song, "Route 66" by Nat King Cole and others, along with the TV show, added to the mystique that still survives to this day. The Interstate Highway 40 bypassed the towns and left them to crumble and decay. Some have survived and have a cult following. Europeans flock to the Highway each summer and travel the road, infatuated with its history. I drove the road a few years back and found it fascinating. Today, it is a Lost Highway, with only portions left to remind us of its legend.

Another lost highway was a song sung by the late, great Hank Williams. Just another guy on the Lost Highway of life, who left us at age 29. Hank, was without a doubt, a troubled soul, whose poetry in song still fits in this modern world. Hank was struggling at the end because of drug and alcohol abuse making his performances few and far between. His legacy in song has made millions for his family, but he never got to enjoy the fruits of his labor. Many of us have found ourselves on the Lost Highway of life. Some, like Hank, never find an exit, and spend their days in misery and despair. Like Hank, they are destined to a life of fruitless dreaming and frustration. We are all familiar with celebrities who rise like a shooting star and then crash back to earth in the style of Hank Williams. Racers we have known fill a long list of tragic career-ending lifestyles that parallel Hank's tragic tale. The Lost Highway has claimed a lot of lives.

Midget racing is a prime example of the Lost Highway syndrome. Rising like a rocket to national acclaim during the 1930s and 1940s, Midget racing owned the spotlight of the sporting public. It was on the high road and seemed to be going to last forever. However, it fell into many problems that left it on the Lost Highway of the sporting life in this country. Many decades were to pass as it languished along the Lost Highway, just a shadow of its former glory days, when it was the king of sports. Fortunately, for us fans of the sport, Midget racing found an exit on Route 66, right here in Tulsa. Two enterprising Okies set up an event called the Chili Bowl, and the rest is history. Emmet Hahn and Lanny Edwards took a chance and today the Chili Bowl has helped Midget racing get off the Lost Highway and back in the limelight of auto racing. Fans of the sport can now experience a renewed interest across the country in this great form of racing. At Ventura Raceway, my home track, we now have a Midget Division that is providing the fans with what I feel is the best form of short track racing. Midget racing may never become the king it once was, but at least it has gotten off the Lost Highway of life and is heading in the right direction. Thank you Emmet, and Lanny, for helping Midget racing off the Lost Highway.

THUNDERTALK
TOM "THUNDERHEAD" TOUTZ
KING OF THE ROAD

No one before, or anyone since, could moan the blues like Hank Williams. Hank was truly one of the greatest country singers of all time. He was a superstar that rose like a rocket to stardom, only to crash and burn due to drug and alcohol abuse at the age of 29. He, along with Elvis, Marilyn, Janice Joplin, Jimmy Hendricks and many others, fell victim to the celebrity syndrome of booze and drug abuse.

Many years ago, I had the pleasure of talking with Tanya Tucker, for an hour or so. The main topic of discussion was "who was the greatest country singer of all time?" She steadfastly defended her choice of George Jones and my choice for the title role was Hank Williams. It was a very spirited discussion, as we both made what we felt a winning argument, and deservingly so. One of her points was that George is still going and Hank died years ago. One of my high points was the song writing and vocal mastery of moanin' the blues held by Hank. It can only be said that both were great artists and we left it as a tie.

Looking back, I have decided that neither of them were truly the greatest country singer of all time. That honor today, in my opinion, would have to be hands down, Willie Nelson. He, not only is the greatest country singer, but also the greatest in all categories of popular music. Now in his 70s, he is still going strong as a singer, song writer, guitar master, author and poet. Six decades of diverse song writing and singing, with a guitar that along with him has transcended many forms of music. These include country, jazz, folk, pop, and blues. I know of no other entertainer that has released 200 albums that truly cover a vast array of musical genres as he has done. This, along with endless travel in his bus, and the Willie Nelson and Family working every type of venue imaginable, has created a true American icon that may never be equaled. He is truly the king of musical entertainers of the last century.

I have also had discussions with a few of my race friends, about who is the greatest race car driver of the last 100 years. It is also a difficult choice to make as many great drivers have ruled as the king over specific periods of time. In reading about the exploits of the early heroes of the sport, one realizes that greatness was usually for a short period of time as the death rate was very high in those early days. Then you have to look at the many forms of racing that have existed over these past years. How many drivers excelled in more than one form of racing, or at least was able to show his abilities in more than one aspect of the sport? This is a short list. Especially today, when upon reaching the upper levels of the sport, contracts come in to play that prohibit such goings on.

Having discussed this subject with many friends and acquaintances, I believe I have come up with the answer to our very difficult question: Who's the king? We discussed, Parnelli Jones, Mario Andretti, A.J. Foyt, and many others too numerous to count in this space. The main deciding factor in my choice was longevity, diversity of driving ability, star power, driving record, championships, and crowd appeal. Thus, it all boiled down to Steve "The King" Kinser. Yes, a true champion over many decades of racing. He, like Willie, still travels the road, entertaining the fans who cheer every time he enters the track. Always there to sign autographs, which has made both men legendary icons in American history.

THUNDERTALK
TOM "THUNDERHEAD" TOUTZ
OUTLAW

Our history is filled with tales of famous outlaws who roamed and robbed after the Civil War and continued through the Great Depression. Frank and Jesse James, the Dalton Gang and Billy the Kid rode roughshod over the country. During the depression, Bonnie and Clyde, Pretty Boy Floyd, John Dillinger and others robbed banks and killed countless people on their reckless rampages. It is interesting, that the movie makers made heroes out of these evil people, when in reality, they were basically the scum of the earth. Suddenly, it was okay to be an outlaw, at least the fantasy version that the press and movie people created. So the term 'outlaw' became an endearing term when used to describe those who worked outside the norm of social standards.

Back in the '70s, Willie Nelson, Waylon Jennings, Kris Kristofferson, David Allen Coe, and a few others formed what was called the Outlaw Movement in country music. Going against the established music powers in Nashville and doing their own thing, it became a legendary sound and style of music that is still popular today. They were a group of mavericks that created a persona that grabbed their fans attention.

Race drivers who traveled and picked big money shows were also mavericks of their time. They had the talent and could ride into town and steal the show. They were true outlaws in every sense of the word. Ted Johnson, who I consider to be one of the few great promoters in the history of Sprint Car racing, recognized the outlaw movement and capitalized on it big time. He created the World of Outlaws, a band of roving renegades who came to town and took the money. Of course,

---

today they are more like Ringling Brothers Circus, a big show that sells out everywhere they go, still outlaws, but a softer version.

There is one driver who stood out as a true outlaw for his entire career. Gary Wright, the "Texan" who spent many seasons running any car, any time. He raced Modifieds, Late Models, Midgets, 410 and 360 Sprint Cars, and NASCAR. With over 400 feature wins to his credit, covering many types of race cars, he truly followed the Outlaw motto and ran anywhere, at any time, always looking for the win and finding it more often than not. Retired, inducted into the Sprint Car Hall of Fame, however, he will always be a true Outlaw. Retiring is a difficult thing to do, especially for a racer. That burning desire to win does not go away easily. Here at the Chili Bowl, I have seen many a driver show up, feeding that burning desire, even after retirement. Maybe, just maybe, Gary might slip into Tulsa, and let us see a true master perform here at the Chili Bowl just one more time.

CONCLUSION

Yes, it has been an incredible journey. Retiring, from all of the physical aspects of running a booth at many events per year, has not been an easy task. I will always miss the excitement and energy of opening up for the first day of a major event. The long drives over the Interstates were always enjoyable, as they gave a lot of time for thoughts and ideas to flow across my mind. Just my music and me flowing down the highway, alone, contemplating my world.

Being a vendor at the races revealed many things along the way. First and foremost, has been the friendships developed while working the Thunderhead booth at the many events I attended. The names would be much too long to list, so I can only say thank you for the support and friendship we have shared over time. Of course, those friendships will continue, as I will be going to the races as long as I am able. It is always a pleasure to run into my race friends at these events.

Being a part of the racing world fulfilled a childhood dream, and allowed me to expand my world experience. These past 17 years have given me some insight into the state of the union of our racing world that includes Sprint Cars, Midgets, and Silver Crown cars. There is much going on in our sport that needs attention on our part. The economic situation has affected car counts and fan attendance. This, along with the new technology is making dramatic changes in how our sport will function in the years to come. The world has changed, and the younger generation has much more to choose from for entertainment. This, along with being able to watch events from your couch, has not helped maintain the crowd counts. The major events still seem to draw big crowds, but without the local racing, the future is not bright. I look around and see my generation starting to fade away. Will the younger crowd continue to be an integral part of keeping the sport alive? Or, will it fade away and be just another memory on the "Lost Highway?" We, as race fans, young and old, need to step up to the plate and support our sport in every way possible.

Our National Sprint Car Hall of Fame, to whom the profits from this book will be donated, is a very key element in the future of our sport. Each and every one of us must make it a priority to be a paying member each year, and if able, to make additional contributions. Their mission to "Promote the Future by Preserving the Past," is of paramount importance to the future health of the sport.

Enough said, let's do it! Looking forward to seeing you at the races.

ACKNOWLEDGEMENTS

My journey with Thunderhead, actually began when I was ten years old and watched the Jalopy races on black and white TV, and listened to Dick Lane call the action in vivid detail. It instilled a passion for dirt track racing that followed me throughout my life. It has been a journey that was priceless in all that has unfolded, since that first exposure to the sport.

Along life's path, there have been many people who I have met that had an influence in my journey. The list is too long to cover, so here are just a few that I would like to acknowledge.

As a young man, I met Martin Fischer, who hired me to be a sales rep in northern California. I had worked in the clothing business at the retail level for thirteen years. This move put me on the wholesale side of the clothing industry. Martin's company produced hosiery and imprinted t-shirts under the brand name of Hang Ten and other designer brands. Martin took me under his wing and taught me how to be a creative factor in both design and marketing of these brands. I ended up as the national sales manager. Beyond the creative and marketing lessons, he also taught me a life lesson in being a credible source to all of those I dealt with. Over the years, Martin became a second father to me, and I am indebted to him for his generosity and support. We still talk and visit and as he approaches his 95th birthday. Thank you, Martin, for all of the love and sharing these many years.

I would not be writing this book, if it were not for Jim Naylor, the promoter of Ventura Raceway. I presented the idea of my being a vendor at his raceway with my Thunderhead racing apparel, and he agreed to give it a shot. Most promoters balk at that concept, but Jim could see that it gave the fans the image that his track was more unique than other venues. A few years ago, Jim asked me to write a weekly column for his program. At first, I balked at the thought, as I had never done much writing. He insisted that I give it a try and I did. This mini journey has proved to be a trip that has been both challenging and creatively satisfying. Writing his column opened up a whole world of sharing thoughts and concepts with other racing fans, drivers and crews. It evolved into writing a column for the Chili Bowl program, which has also been well received by those who attend that event. Jim has been a promoter for over thirty years and single handily resurrected Sprint Car racing in Southern California. This book contains my favorite articles from these series. I hope you enjoy them. Thank you, Jim, for all of your support and friendship we have shared over the years.

Before I started Thunderhead, I would travel to northern California for the Winged Sprint Car Speed Week. As I stopped at Petaluma, I was walking up the grandstand looking for a seat. A seat was empty on the isle, and I asked the guy sitting next to it if it was open. He said, "sit down and join us." I did, and thus began a friendship with one of my best friends, Dave Day and his wife Teri. David is an accomplished singer songwriter and with our mutual interest in classic country music, we have formed a bond that is priceless. David is also a walking history book of Sprint Car racing in Northern California. Attending races with David and his wife Teri always makes an evening special. They are truly an example of race fans that follow the sport of Sprint Car and Midget racing nationwide. Thank you, David, for all of the good times, and friendship over all of these years.

Over the past thirty years, I have attended many trade shows associated with the promotional marketing industry of which I am part. Most of these shows feature guest motivational speakers as part of the agenda. This year, I attended a show in Long Beach and they had a guest speaker that sounded like he might be interesting. I was somewhat reluctant to sit in, as one can become a little jaded after many years of hearing similar speakers. Similar speaker, he was not. I was treated to a very dynamic presentation by Erik Wahl, author and world famous graffiti artist. This 60-minute session woke me up, and gave me the inspiration to get this book done and out in the world. Erik is the author of the book "UN think," which I consider a must-read for any and all of us seeking the answer to our creative journey in life. I thank you, Erik, for the wake-up call.

My journey in creating the Thunderhead experience would not be possible without the support and friendship of race fans across the country and around the world. Too many to list by name, they know who they are, and my heartfelt thanks goes out to them. One of the most unique groups of race friends is the "Milan Mafia." This group of "old school characters" from Illinois, showed up every year at the Chili Bowl. They would stop by and harass me with jokes and stories, along with food from their BBQ. Rich and Sue, a couple from Northern California, travel all over in their motor home, following Sprint Car and Midget races. I could always count on them bringing over dinner from their camp site. Not only was it great food, but the friendship that came along with it was priceless. These are just a couple of examples of the type of people who follow the sport. People who enjoy life and the sport, with an enthusiastic outlook.

The completion of my journey would not have been possible without the love and support of my family. Their enthusiasm for my journey to fulfill my life passion has been heartfelt.

TO THE UBERS!

See you on the thunder road!

2016

36409002R00139

Made in the USA
San Bernardino, CA
22 July 2016